Ethelwold and Medieval Music-Drama at Winchester:
The Easter Play, Its Author, and Its Milieu

European University Studies

Europäische Hochschulschriften
Publications Universitaires Européennes

Series XXX
Theatre, Film and Television

Reihe XXX   Série XXX
Theater-, Film und Fernsehwissenschaften
Théâtre, cinéma et télévision

Vol./Band 10

PETER LANG
Berne · Francfort/M. · Las Vegas

George B. Bryan

Ethelwold and Medieval Music-Drama at Winchester

The Easter Play, Its Author, and Its Milieu

PETER LANG

Berne · Francfort/M. · Las Vegas

CIP-Kurztitelaufnahme der Deutschen Bibliothek

Bryan, George B.:
Ethelwold and medieval music-drama at Winchester : the Easter play,
its author, and its milieu / George B. Bryan. – Berne ; Francfort/M. ;
Las Vegas : Lang, 1981.
    (European university studies : Ser. 30, theatre, film and
    television ; Vol. 10)
    ISBN 3-261-04841-7

NE: Europäische Hochschulschriften / 30

PREFACE

In discussing the symbiotic relationship between drama and medieval liturgy, Glynne Wickham aptly observes that "there is no short cut to genuine understanding of the evolution of a process that was at once historical and doctrinal, musical and artistic, evangelistic and monastic."[1] Previous attempts to explain the genesis and transmission of liturgical music-drama without due consideration of all these aspects have been misrepresentative, even those seminal studies, E.K. Chambers's The Mediaeval Stage (1903) and Karl Young's The Drama of the Medieval Church (1933). Wickham urges caution in accepting "the more recent critical pre-conceptions which have their roots in anti-clericalism and scientific scepticism. One or more of these creeds has underlain almost every historical account of the origin and development of drama in the Middle Ages written during the past hundred and fifty years."[2] To question both the methods and the conclusions of Chambers, Young, and their disciples is now commonplace. Dissipating generations of critical obscuration necessitates returning to the fountainhead of medieval drama, the Easter play contained in the Monastic Agreement (Regularis Concordia), a tenth-century monastic custumal written by Ethelwold, Bishop of Winchester (963-84), and to its musical score preserved in the Winchester Troper:

> 51. While the third lesson is being read, four of the brethren shall vest, one of whom, wearing an alb as though for some different purpose, shall enter and go stealthily to the place of the "sepulchre" and sit there quietly, holding a palm in his hand. Then, while the third respond is being sung, the other three brethren, vested in copes and holding thuribles in their hands, shall enter in their turn and go to the place of the "sepulchre," step by step, as though searching for something. Now these things are done in imitation of the angel seated on the tomb and of the women coming with perfumes to anoint the body of Jesus. When, therefore, he that is seated shall see these three draw nigh, wandering about as it were and seeking something, he shall begin to sing softly and sweetly, Quem quaeritis. As soon as this has been sung right through, the three shall answer together, Ihesum Nazarenum. Then he that is seated shall say Non est hic. Surrexit sicut praedixerat. Ite, nuntiate quia surrexit a mortuis. At this command the three shall turn to the choir saying Alleluia. Resurrexit Dominus. When this has been sung he that is seated, as though calling them back, shall say the antiphon Venite et videte locum, and then, rising and lifting up the veil, he shall show them the place void of the Cross and with only the linen in which the Cross had been wrapped. Seeing this the three shall lay down their thuribles in that same "sepulchre" and, taking the linen, shall hold it up before the clergy; and, as though showing that the Lord was risen and was no longer wrapped in it, they shall sing this antiphon: Surrexit Dominus de sepulchro. They shall then lay the linen on the altar.
> 52. When the antiphon is finished the prior, rejoicing in the triumph of

Le Tropaire de Winchester. Bodleian Ms Bodley 775, fol. 17ᵒ-vᵒ.

Reconstructed Text of the Music of the Visitation to the Sepulchre of the Winchester Troper. The heighted neumes are written over the staffs; the melody is rendered in the usual chant notation on the C-staffs. From Dolan, <u>Le Drame liturgique</u>, pp. 28-29.

our King in that He had conquered death and was risen, shall give out the hymn Te Deum laudamus, and thereupon all the bells shall peal. After this a priest shall say the verse Surrexit Dominus de sepulchro right through and shall begin Matins. ...[3]

After this brief interlude of musico-histrionic activity, the regular service of Matins was conducted in the usual manner. The rubrics and music are so simple that their simplicity has concealed the artistic and religious renaissance connected with tenth-century Winchester. Describing that environment and its products, detailing the events that led Ethelwold to formulate the drama, and clarifying some aspects of its production are the tridentine purpose of this book.

Finally this study is an attempt to explore a complex subject in a manner that students and laymen can profitably read but which may also titillate specialists. A word on spelling and presentation of sources is necessary. Medieval names are Anglicized in the text but written in their original form in the notes as a concession to non-classicists. For the same reason English translations are given in the text and original languages reproduced in the notes (when necessary).

My interest in the Middle Ages stems from an undergraduate theatre history course taught by Orlin R. Corey, but Oscar G. Brockett inspired the book and Hubert C. Heffner guided me as I conceived its first version. I am particularly indebted to the Trustees of the British Museum, who opened their treasure chest of research materials to me; to C. D. Higgins of Indiana University, whose drawings clarify some aspects of my discussion; to Veronica C. Richel and Jane P. Ambrose of the University of Vermont, Alan L. Woods of the Theatre Research Institute of the Ohio State University, and Vaile B. Winter, friend and editor, who read the manuscript and offered useful suggestions; to Edward J. Feidner and Wolfgang Mieder, also of the University of Vermont, for their encouragement; and to Margaret Bellamy, my late grandmother, who lovingly and generously financed the research.

Notes

[1] The Medieval Theatre (London: Weidenfeld and Nicolson, 1974), p. 11.

[2] Shakespeare's Dramatic Heritage: Collected Studies in Mediaeval, Tudor and Shakespearean Drama (London: Routledge & Kegan Paul, 1969), p. 3.

[3] The Monastic Agreement of the Monks & Nuns of the English Nation, trans. Thomas Symons (London: Thomas Nelson & Sons, 1953), pp. 49-51.

"... nor is a complete understanding of any man's work possible, without some knowledge of the conditions under which it had its being, of the influences which helped shape its form and inspire its purpose."

---E.K. Chambers

TABLE OF CONTENTS

LIST OF ILLUSTRATIONS

CHAPTER I

TENTH-CENTURY WINCHESTER

When Bishop Ethelwold's monks first performed their Easter drama, Winchester had been an eminent city for over a thousand years. Its foundation was largely a matter of geography. Situated at the junction of several trackways and in the natural corridor between two great forests, Winchester attracted Neolithic and Iron Age settlers (c. 700-500 B.C.) as well as ancient Celts, who established homesites in what came to be described as Wessex. The area was watered by the River Itchen, which "spread out on a wide belt of hard chalk and flint to give a crossing scarce ankle deep."[1]

Turning their eyes on Britain in 55 B.C., the Romans found a city named Caer Gwent, meaning either White City (because of the neighboring chalk downs) or Market City, inhabited by Celtic Belgae, a race of people skilled in metal and enamel work and possessed of a considerable culture. After subjugating the indigenous Celts, the Romans set about constructing the city they would inhabit for nearly four hundred years. They built two main streets perpendicular to each other and crossing in the center; the present High Street lies along the Roman east-west axis. Then the legions of Caesar circumvallated the city and provided four gates located at the cardinal points of the compass. Five major roads converged at Wintonia, as the Romans called their town. "It was a period in which the whole population of Winchester, and the area around, must have become thoroughly Latinized; as Roman as the Romans in speech and social habit."[3] The old city maintained its agricultural and wool-growing activities throughout the Roman occupation.

The period between the recall of the Roman army in the fifth century and the first mention of Wintonceastre in the entry for 648 in the Anglo-Saxon Chronicle is of unclear definition. Perhaps marauding Saxons appropriated the city deserted by the Romans, but it was many years before they built Wintonceastre on the ruins of the Roman city. The present cathedral rests above one of the Roman streets.[4] The Chronicle states that in 648 Cenwalch, son of Cynegils, built a great church and monastery in Wintonceastre.[5] The erection of these religious precincts signalled "the deliberate choice of Winchester as the centre, ultimately, not only of the shire of which it was as near as possible the geographical centre, but also of the whole kingdom of the Gewissas, or West Saxons."[6]

The Bishopric of Winchester and the Viking Raids

When the church was completed in 676, Bishop Hedda moved the episcopal seat from Dorchester to Winchester, along with precious relics and treasures,[7] thus formally endowing Winchester as one of the most important cities in the Anglo-Saxon heptarchy. Later the monastery was strengthened and a royal palace built, but the accomplishments of the seventh century nearly were obliterated by the contentions of the eighth.

In the eighth century the kingdom of Mercia, under Ethelred, Ethelbald and Offa, captured the dominance exercised by Northumbria in the seventh. Early in the ninth century the balance of power again shifted as Egbert, crowned king of the West Saxons in 802,[8] overwhelmed Beornwulf, Offa's successor in Mercia; Northumbria then acknowledged him overlord. As lord of Wessex, Mercia, and Northumbria, Egbert was crowned king of the English in Winchester in 826; afterward Winchester remained the undisputed capital of the realm, and Egbert emerged as progenitor of all the succeeding English kings except Cnut, the two Harolds, and William I.

Egbert, having extended the borders of Wessex into Cornwall and annexed Kent, divided greater Wessex into relatively autonomous parcels of land called hundreds, each presided over by an ealdorman (alderman). This plan of organization provided a defensive system that shielded Wessex from the worst ravages of the Vikings. In Charlemagne's court Egbert noticed and appreciated the efficient administration of the Kingdom of the Franks, an approach which he imitated in the days when Wessex included all England south of the Thames.

Expeditious response to Viking incursion was a harsh necessity, for the Northmen had plundered Dorset in 787 and Lindisfarne in 793. Egbert mustered a sizeable army but had no navy, so the persistent Danes eventually occupied several coastal towns. Their raids became bloodier during the reign of Ethelwulf, Egbert's son. Havoc and tumult followed the raiders, who eventually penetrated as far inland as Winchester,[9] where in 860 they destroyed everything but the monastery, preserved only because Abbot Swithun built a great wall of flint-rubble around the minster. The city then followed the abbot's example and similarly fortified the town, thus enabling Winchester to survive subsequent raids until the eleventh century.

The Reign of Alfred

Ethelwulf was succeeded by three sons, Ethelbald, Ethelbert, and Ethelred, who ruled and died within fourteen years of one another, each harried by increasingly barbaric Viking sorties. Thereafter Alfred (849-99), called "the Great," was crowned at Winchester and kept his royal court there when he was not campaigning or progressing throughout his realm. A remarkable man was Alfred - ruler, soldier, diplomat, artisan, and teacher. After facing the Vikings in several battles, Alfred succeeded in arranging an inglorious cease-fire; a money payment insured that the Danes would retreat to the east and north of England, an area known as the Danelaw, and cease their attacks upon the West Saxons. For five years the uneasy truce held, while Alfred regrouped his forces, reorganized his defenses, and conceived a rotation scheme whereby half his militia remained at home to tend the crops while the other half defended the kingdom. [10]

Meanwhile the Vikings, some thriving in the security of peaceful existence, others eager to resurrect their belligerance, became factionalized, but when Guthrum assumed command of the troops, attacks upon Wessex began anew. Each battle was followed by treaties and gold payments which served only to veil treachery in other places. Finally the entire Saxon army was routed during a surprise attack at Chippenham in 878. Alfred escaped with a small contingent into the marshes, from which he directed guerrilla attacks upon his enemies. History has dwelt upon his romantic adventures during this time in the wilderness, but his true nobility was demonstrated after his daring victory over the Vikings. When the whole situation seemed the blackest, Alfred stirred from his hideaway in the fens, summoned his militia, and pounced upon the Danes at Ethandun, catching them wholly by surprise and bringing them down. Toward Guthrum Alfred was compassionately condescending. He received his onetime adversary as a vanquished brother, sponsored his baptism as a Christian, became his godfather, and called Guthrum his son. Winston Churchill's evaluation of Alfred's conduct is indicative of Alfred's accomplishment: "This sublime power to rise above the whole force of circumstances, to remain unbiased by the extremes of victory or defeat, to persevere in the teeth of disaster, to greet returning fortune with a cool eye, to have faith in men after repeated betrayals, raises Alfred far above the turmoil of barbaric wars to his pinnacle of deathless glory."[11]

Fourteen years of peace enabled Alfred to initiate those projects to which the mind and spirit are indebted. Alfred codified the earliest set of English laws, a combination of those of Ine, king of Wessex (688-94), and his own pronouncements, and housed the document, the Codex Wintoniensis (the Winchester Book) in St. Swithun's Priory in Winchester. Apart from religion, the king was interested primarily in learning and the arts, but not for the privileged classes alone; he dreamed of instructing the masses, but the traditional teachers, the monks, were abysmally ignorant themselves, as Alfred's earliest biographer Asser records:

> I would have you informed that it has come into my remembrance what wise men there formerly were among the English race, both of the sacred orders and the secular; and what happy times those were throughout the English race. . . . how foreigners came to this land for wisdom and instruction. . . . So clean was it fallen away in the English race that there were very few on this side Humber who could understand their Massbooks in English, or translate a letter from Latin into English; and I ween that there were not many beyond the Humber. [12]

Even when allowances are made for Asser's adulation of Alfred, the situation of the church, and hence of learning, seems irreparably grim; nor was such ignorance dispelled in the tenth century. Indeed, it was magnified. Alfred's first task, then, was to educate his teachers, the monks. To this end he gathered the ablest of scholars, some native Englishmen, some aliens. Plegmund, who became Archbishop of Canterbury in 890; Werferth, Bishop of Worcester after 873; Werwulf, a member of Werferth's staff; and a priest named Athelstan -- these were the king's English educational reformers. The foreign contingent included Grimbald, a monk of St. Bertin's at St. Omer. Another monk called John the Old Saxon directed the activities of a community of monks at Athelney, but his effectiveness was slight because he goaded the brothers so persistently that they tried to murder him. The most familiar name among Alfred's advisers is that of Asser, a monk of St. David's. From these men Alfred learned to read enough Latin and English to see five classical philosophical treatises translated from the classical tongue to the Saxon. Whether he actually did the translating (as some believe) or merely patronized the undertaking is irrelevant; that these Englishings form the basis of Anglo-Saxon prose literature secures Alfred a high place in the history of English letters.

Alfred encouraged a renascence not only of religion, the arts, and literature, but of historiography as well. At the king's behest, the Anglo-Saxon Chronicle, a record of significant events in English history from about A.D. 494, was begun at Winchester. Later chroniclers maintained the annals until 1154.

In spite of his scholarly bent, Alfred was forced to turn from his studies and schemes to face the Vikings once again in 892, and again the raiders capitulated. Death came to the great king in 899. He was buried temporarily in the Old Minster (formerly St. Swithun's Priory) in Winchester till the New Minster, his crowning architectural glory, was completed. Alfred's reign was a prelude to the glories of the tenth-century reawakening.

Alfred's Successors and the 10th-Century Reawakening

Alfred was succeeded first by his son Edward the Elder (899-924?), then by his grandson Athelstan (924?-39) and Edmund (939-46), who ruled while the Danes reconquered the lands secured by Alfred, the Irish-Norse coalition hammered at the northwest, and the Scots threatened in the north. Because of these pressures, especially the Viking sorties, the early tenth century was one of the most dismal periods of English history. Religion and government were ineffective and riddled with abuse; social institutions faltered, and some collapsed because of the state of perpetual warfare. F. M. Stenton does not exaggerate when he says, "There can be no question that the Danish invasions of the ninth century shattered the organization of the English church, destroyed monastic life in eastern England, and elsewhere caused distress and anxiety which made the pursuit of learning almost impossible."[13] These hostilities continued throughout the first half of the tenth century until Edred (946-55), king of Wessex, successfully braved the Viking warriors.

Edred's reign is characterized by repeated attempts to repulse Viking coalitions in the north of England. He eventually made it clear that the English state could preserve its territorial integrity by repelling foreign adventurers bent on colonization. His final act as king, however, was to bequeath a substantial sum of money with which to buy peace; several years passed before the appeasement funds were employed for that purpose.

King Edred died without issue, so the sons of his brother Edmund -- Edwig (aged 15) and Edgar (aged 12) -- stood nearest in line to the throne. Edwig, known in the chronicles as "all-fair" because of his winsome looks, became king and distinguished himself by intemperance and ineptitude. There was little mourning when he died after an unsettled reign of three years, a period in which, nevertheless, there were some important developments.

Edwig's rule marked the beginning of the first time in over a hundred years when England was not faced with the threat of foreign invasion. From the time of Edwig's succession (955) until 980, England enjoyed a period of reconstruction of society, re-establishment of government, and reformation of religious life, with its concomitant re-invigoration of the arts. During this period, Edwig surrounded himself with talented functionaries, whose gifts graced later reigns as well.

The primary accomplishment of the period 955-80, however, is the revival of English monasticism, which effected a rebirth of English culture. Although he was not a zealous adherent of monastic reform, Edwig's gifts to monasteries, "though few, are numerous enough to show that neither he nor the men who influenced him were hostile to monasticism as an institution."[14] On the other hand, Edwig strongly animadverted Dunstan, then Abbot of Glastonbury, later to be Archbishop of Canterbury and a leader of the Monastic Revival.

Some time after 954, the West Saxons, the Mercians, and possibly the Northumbrians swore fealty to Edwig, thus making him ruler of a more or less united kingdom. For reasons not wholly clear, however, the Mercians and the Northumbrians declared their allegiance to Edwig's brother Edgar in 957. The country had two kings for a time, but Edwig's timely death in 959 resulted in Edgar's being accepted as King of the English.

Edgar (957-75) made few governmental changes, but his decisions on ecclesiastical polity were far-reaching and politically-based: Dunstan, exiled by Edwig, was recalled to England and consecrated Bishop of Worcester and London. With him came numerous Flemings whom he had met during his banishment in Ghent. [15] After deposing Byrhthelm, the Archibishop of Canterbury, Edgar installed Dunstan in that office, thus laying the foundation of the Monastic Revival and earning for the king the reputation of being a friend to religion. "In fact, King Edgar hastened into a large-scale spoliation of the lands of the English nobility in the interests of the Church."[16]

It must be admitted, moreover, that Edgar preserved the English peace, established a standard of civil order, and contributed to the development of English culture by supporting the reformation of the English religious houses. He was the first English king to be crowned according to a fixed coronation order; homage from eight British kings acknowledged his supremacy. Wisely Edgar recognized as a separate ethnic entity the Danes residing in the east to England, although he continued to control certain internal affairs. Edgar's reign, then, was an important one.

When Edgar died suddenly in 975, the succession was left in an uncertain state. Having married twice, Edgar was survived by two sons, Edward and Ethelred, one by each wife. Neither was old enough to assume control, and the records are cryptic about the events that followed the king's death, but partisan spirit was violent. Even after Edward's coronation in 975, the threat of civil war was abiding.

Edward's disgusting speech habits and behavior were petty faults when compared with his ambivalence toward the newly-strengthened monasteries. That Edward was hostile to the religious houses cannot be substantiated, but that he was especially concerned lest the monasteries gain control of vast parcels of land is certain. King Edward supported the claims of nobles who held hereditary deeds to lands then possessed by the monks. The landlordship of the great religious houses weakened the authority of the nobles of the shires, upon whom the king depended for the maintenance of peace and order. These very nobles, furthermore, watched the fortunes of their heirs disappear as more and more land was granted to the monks. Their dissatisfaction is understandable.

Edward was murdered in 978/9 under mysterious circumstances, which suggests the complicity of members of Ethelred's retinue; thus Ethelred commenced his reign under a cloud of suspicion, and the crown lost the respect of many adherents. Edward the Martyr was created a saint, an act which focused attention on Ethelred as a saint-killer. Thereafter, Ethelred's reign (978/9-1013/4), characterized by suspicions, military ineptitude, and poor relations with nobility and peasantry alike, was punctuated by renewed Danish invasions after 980. The Danish clans had been united under a single king since the middle of the tenth century, and by 980 political conditions in Denmark caused many of the bolder Danes to seek to colonize England in order to escape an autocratic government and an imposed state religion.

The Viking raids, although severe in a given locale, at first held little consequence for England as a whole, except for a mutual aid treaty imposed by Pope John XV upon Ethelred and Duke Richard I of Normandy. [17] By 991 the Danish attacks became so overwhelming that a heavy tax was levied throughout England to raise money to buy off the invaders. Bargaining and battles continued thereafter with growing ferocity until England was brought to its knees and Cnut the Dane became joint king of England and Denmark in 1016.

That several fortunate events coalesced to make the early English theatre possible is implicit in the foregoing narration. The establishment of Winchester as governmental, ecclesiastical, and cultural center endowed the ancient city with honors and rendered possible the appearance there of important innovations in several fields. The brief twenty-five year period of peace was a time of reconstruction and revivification of humanistic arts, among them the creation of drama, all of which were encouraged by Edgar's reforming zeal. Thus, in that sense, politics contributed to the rise of drama; that societal organization affected the arts is also demonstrable.

The Structure of 10th-Century Society: The Ceorls

Town and country life in tenth-century England, that is, in market towns and agricultural manors, was circumscribed by rigid custom which was marked by local and regional ambiguities. Describing these societal structures is fraught with contradictions and confusions that result from these ambiguities. Despite these difficulties of language, usage, and custom, it is necessary to set forth some aspects of life in the <u>ports</u> (market towns) and <u>vills</u> (agricultural estates).

A fundamental distinction was made between freemen and slaves, the latter being considered mere chattel and the object of the church's charity. Social classes were differentiated (1) by the amount of <u>wergild</u> (man-worth in gold) exacted from a killer in behalf of the heirs of a murdered man; (2) by the value attached to their oaths; (3) by the compensation paid as the result of an injury; and (4) by taxes and fines they ordinarily paid. The slave had no <u>wergild;</u> his master, rather than his heirs, received the compensatory fine for his injury or death; his life was worth sixty shillings, although his longevity frequently was cut short because many minor infractions of the law were punishable by death or mutilation. The number of slaves in England varied periodically; there were nearly 30,000 in 1086, the year of the Domesday survey. The original slaves probably were the early Britons who met the invading Angles, Saxons, and Jutes. A child born in serfdom remained in servitude unless he were manumitted. The slave population was augmented by captives taken during insular wars, children sold by parents for ready cash, and criminals who had lost their rights while expiating certain crimes. The slave's dream of being freed was ever-present, even while he was being bought and sold like livestock. [18] Naturally the lot of slaves varied from region to region, and serfs on church estates normally fared better than their opposites on secular manors. Doubtless, then, some slaves desired to enter the church as priests and monks; some actually did so, but it was unusual. Since the slaves attended religious services in chapels on the estates, the only way in which they might witness the production of music-dramas in the monastic cathedrals was through their admission to the monastery as oblates.

A description of the English freeman is more difficult to formulate. Initially the class of freemen included earls (nobility) and ceorls (commons), each of whom owned his land through a charter issued by the king. The class of earls was comprised of the king, the royal family, the hereditary nobles, and upper clergy, such as archbishops, bishops, and certain abbots. The distinction between ceorls and other freemen was based on whether land was held through royal charter (as with the ceorls) or through commission of oneself to the service and protection of a landlord. Speculation about these classes is derived primarily from four documents: an account book of the ceorls of Hurstbourne Priors, a monastic manor in Hampshire owned by the monks of Winchester,[19] a survey of an estate in Gloucestershire,[20] a handbook of estate management called "Rights and Ranks of the People,"[21] and a bailiff's guidebook entitled "On Discriminating Stewards."[22]

> At Hurstbourne Priors (called Eisseburn in Old English), the ceorls were required to pay their lord forty pence a year from every hide [a unit of land measure], specified but now uncertain quantities of ale, wheat, and barley, to plough three acres of their lord's land in their own time and sow them with their own seed, to mow half an acre of meadow, to supply specified amounts of wood and fencing, to wash and shear their lord's sheep in their own time and to work on their lord's lands as they were bidden every week in the year except three, one at midwinter, the second at Easter and the third at the Rogation Days."[23]

Thus, a rather clear picture of peasant activities emerges, and it is rendered more valuable since life on a manor regulated by the monks of Winchester is described. Of such stock, Chambers and his followers suggest, the audience of the liturgical music-drama was composed. Actually, in only one instance would these ceorls have been in attendance when the play was performed: if they had elected to become monks.

The workers at Tiddenham,[24] a vill in Gloucestershire owned by the abbey at Bath, made a considerable part of their living by fishing; from their catches the lord received one fish out of every two and every rare fish. The term "ceorl" does not appear in the survey of Tiddenham; rather, the husbandmen are designated geneat, gebur, and cotsela, who did not own their own land as did the ceorls. These classes of workmen were technically freemen, but they held their land only as a result of serving a landlord. These husbandmen, wherever they lived, would have had few opportunities to leave the manor. It is unlikely that they ever saw the cathedral in their diocese; hence they could not have witnessed monastic plays.

The two remaining documents deal with the direction of an ideal estate and probably were written as a single compendium. Once again the peasants are called geneatas and geburs, the former serving as escorts, lords' bodyguards, dispatch riders, harvesters, and travelers throughout the countryside in the lords' interests. Thus the geneat held a rather responsible position as a companion to a greater man. The gebur was considerably lower in the social hierarchy, and agricultural work occupied most of his time. In these treatises appears the cotsela, a freeman who worked for his lord every Monday and three days a week at harvest time. He paid no rent and farmed as little as five acres for himself. The cotsela was dependent entirely upon the lord for his support. The paucity of agricultural duties prescribed for the cotsela suggests that he may have served the lord as an agent-in-residence on the estate and discharged menial duties for his master.

On a great manor there were specialized workers, such as bee-keepers, swineherds, and shepherds -- sometimes slaves, often freemen. Superintending all the workers for the landlord was the bailiff, or reeve, who served as farm manager. The reeve knew the intricacies of farming and herding, planting and reaping the crops, buying supplies, and maintaining the multifarious tools required for the functioning of the manor.

Even though "Rights and Ranks of the People" and "On Discriminating Stewards" deal with hypothetical manors, their revelations are perhaps applicable to estates throughout tenth-century England. The major source of evidence about actual estates is the great Domesday Book, a survey of all the lands of England initiated by William the Conqueror in 1085 and completed in 1086. "So very thoroughly did he have the inquiry carried out that there was not a single hide, not even one virgate of land, not even -- it is shameful to record it, but it did not seem shameful for him to do -- not even one ox, nor even one cow, nor one pig which escaped notice in this survey. And all the surveys were subsequently brought to him": so reads the Anglo-Saxon Chronicle for the year 1085.

Wessex did not escape the great census, and from the Hampshire Domesday may be deduced that the term villein roughly corresponds to gebur and bordar to cotsela. [25] Out of a population of approximately 1,800,000 in all England in 1086 (since the census-takers counted only heads of houses and owners of property--and not monks, nuns, children, and wives --, an accurate count is impossible), around 10,373[26] resided in Hampshire. Of these, thirty-seven per cent were villeins, while thirty-eight per cent were bordars; thus, most of the inhabitants were connected with the agricultural economy. Sixteen and one-half per cent of the people were serfs, a number that was twice the national average. The earls numbered about four per cent, while town-dwellers amounted to two and three-fourths per cent of the total population. [27] If lay-people were admitted to dramatic presentations in the Old Minster (which is not likely), there was a potential city congregation of about two hundred eighty-five.

The Earls

The political and fiscal administration of the country was controlled by the group of earls, with the thegns on the lowest rung of the social ladder and the king on the highest. Thegns were freemen who initially inherited their office as companions of the king. [28] They normally held lands by royal charter but also through grants from higher nobility, bishops, or abbots. Their duties included military service (fyrdfaereld), repair of fortifications (burhbot), and the maintenance of bridges (brycegeweorc). Thegns were also responsible for helping to equip the navy, keeping the coastal watch, acting as bodyguards to the king, and serving in the local militia. Thegns kept the king's peace in their own neighborhoods.

A higher official than the thegn, the king's reeve was charged with the management of royal estates, the exercise of justice at the hundred-courts, collecting fines, detaining prisoners, arranging executions, acting as witness at purchases, helping to collect church tithes, and assisting abbots in secular affairs. [29] In towns the reeve had some special responsibilities such as supervising mints, overseeing trade, collecting tolls, witnessing purchases, and conducting ordeals. Town reeves, such as those in Winchester, were not answerable to the ealdormen, their superior officers; they had direct access to the king.

Ealdormen (literally "older men") were the king's deputies and were entrusted with the governance of the shires or even provinces. They were instructed to dispense justice in the county courts, supervise coiners, and help the bishops protect the privileges of the church. Ealdormen, sometimes members of the royal family, sat on the great council of the kingdom.

As to the position of the king, Whitelock observes,

> [T]he king was in a unique position at law. His mere word was incontrovertible, and he need not support it with an oath. An attempt on his life, whether directly, or by harbouring his enemies and outlaws, cost life and all possessions.... If anyone fought in the king's house, he forfeited all that he possessed, and his life was at the king's mercy. [30]

The king's decisions were made often in consultation with his great council, composed of ealdormen, bishops, important abbots, some thegns, and sometimes priests, especially those of his own household and secretariat. King Edred's will enumerates rewards granted to his personal staff: a seneschal, a keeper of the wardrobe, a butler, a chaplain, other priests, and stewards, [31] all of which offices were extremely prestigious and sometimes filled by high-ranking courtiers.

A final word about the kingship is fitting. The assumptions undergirding the monarchy were always in flux during the tenth century. Once the king had been merely the chief warrior among equal chiefs. When Charlemagne was crowned emperor by the pope, he embodied a new interpretation of the kingship in the West, that of being God's emissary on earth. After Charlemagne's passing, kings repeatedly stressed their election by God, and that belief grew into the doctrine of "the divine right of kings." England had been influenced in many ways by the management of Charlemagne's empire, not the least of which was this concept

of the king as chief-priest. Charlemagne had not invented this concept; he merely imported it from Byzantium, and through him it reached England. Edgar's coronation rite has been mentioned. The author of that ceremony, Dunstan, stressed
the divine element of kingship by delaying Edgar's coronation until his twenty-
ninth birthday, the age at which Jesus began his public ministry. An examination
of this ritual reveals several comparisons between the newly-raised king and the
King of Kings. Finally, Edgar began to style himself basileos Anglorum, king of
the Angles, but he used the Greek word which suggests a royal priesthood, rather
than the Latin rex. [32] Edgar was not the first English king to style himself in this
manner, but with him it was usual rather than exceptional. This emulation of
Byzantine culture will be alluded to again in another context.

These strata of society are placed in clearer perspective by a Northumbrian document called "The Wergild of Partcular Persons among the English,"[33]
which had a counterpart (now lost) in Wessex. According to this essay, a king's
wergild is 30,000 thrimsas (a thrimsa amounted to three pennies); archbishops
or athelings (royal princes) are worth 15,000 thrimsas; bishops and ealdormen,
8,000; holds (a Scandinavian equivalent of high reeves) or king's high reeves,
4,000; priests and thegns, 2,000; and ceorls, 266 thrimsas. The ceorls who became priests rose in the social hierarchy to the class of mass-thegns. This document may also suggest that priests were often of upper-class stock, which
agrees with what is known of the secular clerks who figure so prominently in the
story of Ethelwold's reformation of the monasteries at Winchester.

The king and his retinue periodically traversed the countryside to enjoy
the hospitality of his underlings and to inspect his many estates, such as Ched-
dar. The ceorls seldom left these estates, the enjoyment of travel being denied
them. The countryside was their domain, and it played a more modestly important role in the lives of town-dwellers. The burgesses of a great city like Winchester were involved in supplying the needs of the administrative and ecclesiastical capital as well as producing goods and services needed by the agrarian
economy. [34]

The Borough of Winchester

All the English towns were royal establishments, which distinguished
English towns from continental cities. "Although by the end of the Saxon period," writes Whitelock, "other persons might own property and rights in the
boroughs, in general the burgesses held their tenements at a fixed rent from the
king...."[35] The town-dwellers also had certain ties to the land, normally possessing arable fields, communal pastures, and meadows, the care of which was
entrusted to a few individuals.

[T]he average Anglo-Saxon town probably presented a somewhat rural
aspect; there were crofts and gardens within and around the walls, and

many citizens possessed cattle which they pastured on the common of the town. There were several corn mills inside the town; ...the tenth-century boundaries of a small site in Winchester include the west mill, the east mill, and the old mill. [36]

The scarcity of contemporary records precludes a precise description of the nature of Anglo-Saxon towns, but two documents known as the "Burghal Hidage" and the "Winton Domesday," augmented by recent archaeological excavations, reveal some aspects of medieval Winchester.

Winchester had been the chief city of Wessex for hundreds of years when the Easter music-drama was presented in the Old Minster. Alfred the Great commenced the fortifications of the town, and during the reign of Edward the Elder (899-924), the "Burghal Hidage"[37] was drawn up. The document describes defense precautions, and from it one discovers that Winchester contained 2,400 hides, a land measure of somewhat less than forty acres; 2,400 men were required to defend the city. Since there were nowhere near that many urban inhabitants, defenders were recruited in the countryside. The ramparts measured six hundred poles, or a little under two miles, the precise length of the walls of Roman Wintonia. In area Winchester and Wallingford were the largest cities of Wessex. These military requirements became congruent with commercial considerations in the middle of the century, as Blair notes:

> War or the threat of war was seldom absent from tenth-century England and in such conditions there would be profit to the merchant in the form of recongnized markets and to the king in the form of greater tolls if trade could be directed to particular centres and thereby brought under some measure of control, directed in other words to the burh, or, to use a term which emphasises the mercantile rather than the military aspect of what may have been one and the same place, to the port. [38]

Edward the Elder allowed no commercial activities except in market towns (such as Winchester) under the supervision of a port-reeve. Later kings (Edgar, for instance) superintended commerce in a similar manner but condoned trading outside towns as well. The picture of Winchester which emerges, therefore, is one of a thriving commercial city populated by governmental and ecclesiastical functionaries and the craftsmen and artisans necessary to their support, a picture that is corroborated by the "Winton Domesday."

Although William I's domesday survey of Winchester is not extant, two censuses of the town were conducted in later reigns. Henry I (1100-35) desired precise information about his holdings in Winchester. To superintend the eighty-six burgesses who managed the survey, Henry appointed the bishop of Winchester and four courtiers. These listers visited every dwelling, shop, and site in town, and the results of their tally appeared around 1110. A second survey was instigated in 1148 for slightly different reasons. The special characteristics of Winchester as a royal city are reflected in both censuses, As Martin Biddle ob-

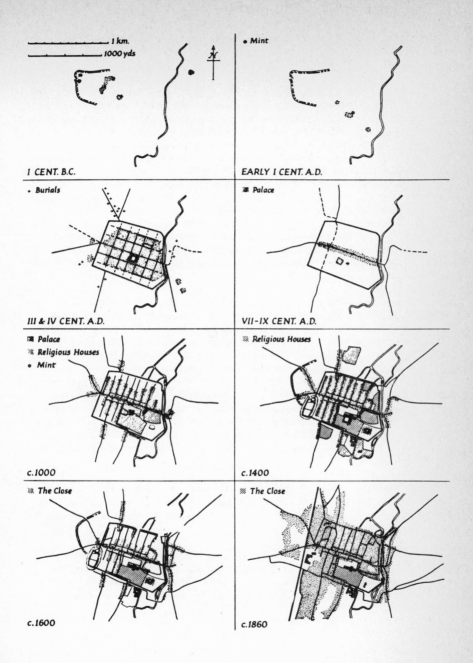

Fig. 1. The Growth of Winchester

serves, "Winchester, the seat of the treasury and the headquarters of so many royal clerks and sergeants, had every stimulus to develop its good geographical position as a trading and industrial centre. "[39]

On the basis of his archaeological findings in Winchester, Biddle calls the Old English city "a royal and ecclesiastical centre without equal in England and recalling the great complexes at Aachen and Rome. "[40] His reference is, of course, to the Vatican in Rome and to Charlemagne's palatial-religious center at Aix-la-Chapelle. The hub of Winchester was dominated in the tenth century by the Old Minster (the cathedral church and ancient monastery), the New Minster, and Nunnaminster (all separated from the city by a high wall),[41] the king's palace, the bishop's palace, nearly a dozen parish churches, among them St. Gregory's, St. Maurice's, the "Wind" Church, St. Peter's, St. George's, St. Mary's, and St. Michael's,[42] and all the outbuildings necessary to temporal and spiritual government. In addition, the treasury offices were housed in Winchester, as well as six moneyors, or mints.[43] An added dimension of munificence was created by the designation of the Old Minster as the royal burial place of kings Cenwalch and Alfred (later removed to the New Minster), as well as of SS. Birinus and Swithun.[44]

The nature of guilds in tenth-century Winchester has not been determined, but it is probable that flourishing trade prompted the founding of a guild merchant in 856, following which several others were formed.[45] By the eleventh century many crafts and trades were practiced, a number of which gave their names to streets. The "Winton Domesday" notes tailors, shieldmakers, tanners, shoewrights, fishmongers, goldsmiths, and fleshmongers -- to name but a few.[46] The king collected rents from sixty-three burgesses living on the High Street alone. Some city properties were worth more than an entire country estate. Several buildings were held by priests presumably attached to the royal and episcopal courts. The city of Winchester paid the king eighty pounds annually for his "aid" or protection; only London paid a sum in excess of this. The survey also shows that there was a newly-created market near the walls of the three monasteries.[47]

The manufacture of cloth[48] and parchment[49] was the main commercial pursuit of Winchester, and as a result of these interests, land inside the city walls was extremely valuable. In 957-58 the Old Minster traded twelve country hides for two city acres.[50]

Thus, to the picture of a relatively populous, sprawling city devoted to government, religion, and commerce must be added the features of wealthy burghers, bureaucrats, masters and apprentices in several trades, all contributing to the life of the kingdom and yet maintaining both civic and rural aspects.

The Church in Winchester

The city of Winchester, along with the remainder of England, was dominated by king and church, the nature of which must be limned as the backdrop against which Ethelwold's drama was played. The traditional hierarchical structure of the Roman Catholic Church, with some insular modifications inspired by Celtic Christianity, obtained in tenth-century England. Remarkable advancement was made at that time in spite of nearly constant warfare. The Bishop of Rome (there were twenty-three, give or take a few anti-popes, during the tenth century),[51] was the titular head of Christendom although the pope's temporal influence was not as great as it became during the Renaissance. His actual power waxed and waned in proportion to the strength of his will and that of his supporters. The pastor of a far-flung, multi-racial flock, the pope claimed to be the spiritual father of the princes and parsons of the church, a group which can be divided into secular and regular clergy.

Secular clerks included most of the archibshops, bishops, archdeacons, and priests, and as their name suggests, they ministered to Christians in secular society. The regular clergy included all those religious who adhered to a common rule of discipline, a regula, hence "regular"; the most obvious regulars were monks and nuns who did the Opus Dei, the Work of God, as an end in itself. The regular clergy were scarcely concerned with the vagaries of secular ministry; their concerns were supra-secular.

Abbot AElfric's tenth-century custumal[52] and the ancient ceremonial of Salisbury Cathedral[53] indicate that seven grades of secular ministers were ordained, each one being a prerequisite of the next: doorkeeper; reader (pronounces the scriptural lesson and preaches); exorcist (conjures accursed spirits in Christ's name); subdeacon (serves the deacon at the altar); deacon (ministers to the mass-priest); and the priest (the celebrant). The holy orders, it should be noted, included these seven and no more. The absence of a separate episcopal order is conspicuous. Viewing the bishop as only a priest set over other priests for administrative efficiency is a tenth-century concept; archbishops were similarly viewed.

The governor of cloistered monks was the abbot, sometimes appointed by the king, often elected by the chapter as a closely guarded privilege. In a community of monks and oblates, a certain number of priests were required for the celebration of the Mass and Divine Office. A man might simultaneously be both monk and priest, but not every monk was a priest, nor was every priest a monk. Certain other officers served monasteries, but hierarchical precedence was not granted them as a rule. The nature of tenth-century monastic life is expressed clearly by a monk in the dialogues of AElfric: "I am a monk by profession and I sing every day the seven services of the hours with my brethren and am occupied with reading and singing, but nevertheless I should like, between times, to learn Latin."[54] AElfric, a disciple of Ethelwold, wrote at the end of the Monastic Revival; the preceding comment shows that the goals of the reawakening were not realized even by the eleventh century. In a monastic community, representatives of all classes of society might be found. Kings abdicated to become monks; widowed queens frequently entered convents. Civic leaders took the cowl, as did Caedmon (a peasant) and Cuthbert (a ceorl).

In tenth-century England a curious circumstance occurred when abbots were created bishops, as was the case with Dunstan, Ethelwold, and others who figure prominently in this story. In the case of each of these men, he was at once the head of a particular monastery (through his abbacy) and the ultimate head of every monastery in his diocese (through episcopacy); he was the spiritual overseer of all the diocesan laity (through his bishopric) and yet unconcerned with the religious welfare of the masses (through his abbacy). The abbot-bishop, furthermore, sat on the great council of the kingdom through being a bishop. His abbacy alone, unless of an important house, would not qualify him to serve as the king's counselor. Finally, as bishop, his see was located in a cathedral church; as abbot, he celebrated the Mass and the Hours in a conventual church, closed generally to lay observance. In the case of the reforming bishops, the monastic church was also the cathedral church, a fact which has important implications for establishing the identity of the audience of the Easter drama. England had the only monastic cathedrals in Europe during the tenth century. [55]

For purposes which shall be apparent presently, the functions of the local priest and bishop should be detailed while deferring a fuller discussion of monastic officers to another chapter. The spiritual director of England's commons was the parish priest, a designation firmly established by the tenth century in deed if not in name. [56] The local vicar (such as those who served the dozen[57] or more churches in Winchester and the one hundred thirty-two[58] on Hampshire farms), with his meager education, was nonetheless in a position to exercise considerable influence on the daily lives of his congregation, since he shared all the workaday and festal experiences of his people. Though priests usually came from the lower ranks of earls or the upper reaches of the ceorls, they were of precisely the same stock and class as most of their neighbors. In the tenth century, the parson normally was married, though the church never officially countenanced a married clergy, and fairly well-off from farming the land deeded to his church. Of course the priest did not actually sow and plow; he hired workers to relieve him of those tasks. Additional income was derived from offerings collected at Mass, plough-alms (an annual penny tax on every parcel of arable land), and burial fees; if his church had a cemetery, the priest was entitled to a fraction of the church tithe. [59]

In addition to dispensing such religious lore as his minimal training allowed and occasionally serving as guild chaplain, the local priest participated in the holidays of his people. Customs codified by Alfred specified that all freemen were to have holidays at Christmas, February 15, March 12, seven days before and seven days after Easter, June 29, a week at harvest time, and November 1. Slaves were released from work on the Wednesdays of the four Ember Weeks. [60]

Local ministers were required to visit the cathedral at least once a year to obtain a supply of the chrism (holy oil), and at that time they were catechized and examined for doctrinal error. Normally the priest said Mass daily and administered the other sacraments as required. If the existence of the priest was commonplace, the life of his superior, the bishop, was glamorous, adventurous, and thoroughly dramatic.

The church and state worked in such political concert in the tenth century that it is difficult to speak separately of ecclesiastical and secular legislation. It has been noted that the king's council included the bishops. In England, unlike on the continent, bishoprics had been established to correspond to tribal, not civic, divisions; consequently, bishops did not become secular potentates of civic and commercial interests at an early date. Only after Wessex became the leading political entity of England did churchmen dabble in politics, and only from the tenth century onward were bishops active in influencing and executing secular legislation. This is largely the contribution of the reforming bishops who engineered the Monastic Revival. By using churchly counselors, the state benefited from the services of the best-educated men in the kingdom, but in some instances the church suffered from a conflict of interests on the part of her bishops.

The bishop, moreover, was the spiritual father of his diocese (the tenth-century designation would have been parochia, or parish, in a much broader sense than in contemporary usage), and in that capacity he served alongside the ealdormen in courts -- and in battle, if necessary. The bishop was defender of his clergy in secular courts, since episcopal courts were not fully empowered until after the Conquest. Many a bishop, nevertheless, exercised a formidable discipline over his clergy through private -- and not always charitable -- means.

A late tenth- or early eleventh-century document, "The Bishop,"[61] enumerates several episcopal responsibilities: actively promoting spiritual and secular rectitude; instructing the priests in his charge; seeking peace and concord; serving in a judicial capacity; overseeing oaths and ordeals; insuring the validity of weights and measures; converting sinners (the bishop is admonished to mingle with his people in order to assess their problems); and encouraging Christian relations between the extremes of society, that is, between the earls and the ceorls.[62] The bishop, therefore, was involved closely with both spiritual and temporal concerns. The impression is not one of a sequestered saint spending his days in manual labor and his nights in fasting and prayer. On the contrary, the tenth-century bishop was at the center of the weighty activities of his day. That the English bishops were daily in contact with all strata of society, even itinerant mimes, jugglers, and other performers, may be an inspiration for the creation of religious drama.

Antecedents of the Monastic Revival

At the close of the tenth century, there were seventeen "parishes" in England; of these, six (Canterbury, Winchester, Sherborne, Worcester, Ely, and Durham) were under the control of monastic bishops, while the remaining eleven were held by seculars. The compilers of the Abingdon Chronicle reported that in 993 there were at least eighteen monasteries in England in addition to the monastic cathedrals: Abingdon, Glastonbury, the New Minster at Winchester, St. Augustine's at Canterbury, Ely, Chertsy, Malmesbury, Bath, Muchelney, Milton (Abbas), Exeter, Athelney, Westminster, Ramsey, Peterborough, and the mysterious minster called the Wind. [63] None of the ancient lists of convents agrees with another, so it is impossible to say exactly how many monasteries lasted until the end of the tenth century, perhaps as many as forty. The story of the success of the monks has its roots in the days of King Alfred.

The church prospered under Alfred's care, although his projections of an educated laity were far from realized. Edward the Elder established three new bishoprics (Wells, Crediton, and Sherborne) and confirmed his father's ecclesiastical statutes which forbade witchcraft, strengthened the civil laws that required payment of church tithes, and established penalties for desecrating the sabbath and holy days. He also completed the building of the New Minster at Winchester and had his father's remains interred there with great pomp. Accordingly, it may be said that the church history of England immediately after Alfred's death centered upon the king rather than upon any of his clerics, and the same observation may be made justifiably of Athelstan's reign, during which a number of ecclesiastical laws were promulgated. [64] The king's monopoly on creative churchmanship was somewhat vitiated when Oda[65] was elevated to the see of Canterbury in the middle of the tenth century.

Oda's accomplishments must be judged in the light of chaotic conditions that necessitated stern measures; his contributions to the English church bore fruit many years after his death. Oda's reforms were the principal forerunners of the Monastic Revival, which, in part, sought to correct the same abuses against which Oda struggled.

Initially the English religious foundation had been entirely monastic, but years of easy living coupled with the urgency of braving the Viking raids enfeebled the monks; the metamorphosis from rigorous spirituality to mundane materialism was so gradual that it passed unnoticed by many. Secular clergy inhabited monasteries abandoned by frantic monks fleeing the onslaught of the Danes. The seculars, who once had subscribed to a rule of sorts, deserted their discipline when they took over the buildings and lands of the monks. Many of the seculars, recruited mostly from the minor nobility, [66] were more interested in expanding their personal fortunes on earth than in laying up treasures in heaven. With their wives they lived in great dissipation in holy places, although the monkish chroniclers probably exaggerated their depravity to magnify the accomplishments of the reformers.

Oda, himself a secular priest, deserted his fellows when the archbishopric was offered to him and declared that only a monk was fit to occupy the see of Canterbury. The most austere and exemplary body of monks then in existence was the Benedictine Order, but there was no community of black monks (so-called because of their black habits) in England at the time. Oda, consequently, applied to St. Benoît-sur-Loire (Fleury), a sisterhouse of Cluny, the fountainhead of continental monastic reform, and received the monastic cowl prior to his enthronement in Augustine's seat in 942. This intercourse with Fleury and continental monasticism held important consequences for the Monastic Revival which followed very shortly.

Oda's first task was restoring and rebuilding the damaged parts of the primatial cathedral in Canterbury; then with the king's collusion he issued some stringent theses: (1) All church property [he declared] is to be free from secular claims, and all appropriated property is to be returned to the church; (2) Kings and princes must recognize bishops as their spiritual superiors; (3) Bishops must actively direct the work of their dioceses and preach frequently; (4) Priests must live exemplary lives before their congregations; (5) All ministers must obey the ancient canons of church law; (6) Monks should remain cloistered and regular; (7) Priests must not marry nuns or close relatives; (8) Everyone should strive to live in concord and amity; (9) Sundays and holidays must be observed strictly; (10) Church tithes must be paid regularly. [67]

Oda sought to correct contemporary abuses in a forceful manner, and the king's complicity lent his pronouncements the power of legality. The archbishop's influence was so pervasive, in fact, that detractors complained that he was turning the palace into a monastery. While Edmund and Edred were on the throne, Oda's reforms proceeded apace, but the situation was altered drastically when Edwig succeeded in 955. What happened then occasioned the movement known as the Monastic Revival and is the subject of the next chapter.

Notes

[1] Walter L. Woodland, The Story of Winchester (London, 1932), p. 5.
[2] Anglo-Saxon Chronicle, anno 60 B.C. The Chronicle hereafter is designated ASC and the edition referred to, if not otherwise indicated, is by Dorothy Whitelock, et al., eds., The Anglo-Saxon Chronicle (New Brunswick, N.J., 1961).
[3] Woodland, p. 18.
[4] Martin Biddle, The Old Minster: Excavations near Winchester Cathedral, 1961-1969 (Winchester, 1970), p. 3.
[5] ASC, anno 648.
[6] Woodland, pp. 24-25.
[7] Woodland, p. 25.
[8] ASC, anno 802.

[9] ASC, anno 860.

[10] ASC, anno 893.

[11] Winston S. Churchill, The Birth of Britain. The History of the English-Speaking Peoples, Vol. I (New York, 1958), p. 117.

[12] Robert H. Hodgkin, A History of the Anglo-Saxons, 2nd ed. (London, 1939), I, 608-609.

[13] F. M. Stenton, Anglo-Saxon England, 2nd ed. (Oxford, 1947), p. 426. Since Stenton is regarded by most specialists in Anglo-Saxon history as a perspicacious scholar, his general assumptions form the basis of my discussion of tenth-century politics.

[14] Stenton, p. 360.

[15] Philip Grierson, "The Relation between England and Flanders before the Norman Conquest," Transactions of the Royal Historical Society, 4th ser., XXIII (1941), 71-112.

[16] Eric John, "Orbis Britanniae and the Anglo-Saxon Kings," Orbis Britanniae and Other Studies (Leicester, 1966), p. 56. Also see H. R. Loyn, "Church and State in England in the 10th and 11th Centuries," Tenth-Century Studies, ed. David Parsons (London, 1975), pp. 94-102.

[17] The text of this document is translated in Dorothy Whitelock, ed., English Historical Documents, c. 500-1042 (London, 1968), pp. 823-824. Whitelock's book is hereafter cited as EHD.

[18] EHD, p. 60.

[19] Joseph Stevens, A Parochial History of St. Mary Bourne, with an Account of the Manor of Hurstbourne Priors, Hants. (London, 1888).

[20] F. W. Maitland, Domesday Book and Beyond (Cambridge, 1897), p. 330.

[21] "Rectitudines sive Singularum Personarum," Ancient Laws and Institutes of England, ed. Benjamin Thorpe (London, 1840), pp. 185-189.

[22] Felix Liebermann, "Gerefa," Anglia, IX (1886), 251-266.

[23] Peter H. Blair, Anglo-Saxon England (Cambridge, 1962), p. 263. Also see English Historical Documents, 1042-1189, ed. David C. Douglas and G. W. Greenaway (London, 1953), pp. 816-817.

[24] Douglas and Greenaway, pp. 817-818.

[25] Dorothy Whitelock, The Beginnings of English Society (Harmondsworth, Eng., 1962), p. 102.

[26] William Page, ed., A History of Hampshire and the Isle of Wight. The Victoria History of the Counties of England (London, 1912), V, 409.

[27] A. H. Inman, Domesday and Feudal Statistics (London, 1900), pp. 3, 5.

[28] H. R. Loyn, Anglo-Saxon England and the Norman Conquest (London, 1962), p. 219.

[29] EHD, p. 66.

[30] Whitelock, p. 50.

[31] EHD, p. 512.

[32] Registrum Hamonis Hethe Diocesis Roffensis, A. D. 1319-1352, ed. Charles Johnson. Canterbury and York Society, No. 41 (Oxford, 1948), I, 32-33.

[33] EHD, pp. 432-433.

[34] J. Tait, The Mediaeval English Borough (Manchester, 1936), p. 119.

32

[35] Whitelock, p. 127.

[36] Whitelock, p. 131.

[37] A. J. Robertson, ed., Anglo-Saxon Charters (Cambridge, 1939), pp. 246-248.

[38] Blair, p. 294.

[39] Martin Biddle, ed., Winchester in the Early Middle Ages: An Edition and Discussion of the Winton Domesday. Winchester Studies, No. 1 (Oxford, 1976), p. 28.

[40] Martin Biddle, "Winchester," Archaeological Journal, CXXIII (1966), 182-183.

[41] Liber Vitae: Register and Martyrology of New Minster and Hyde Abbey, Winchester, ed. Walter de Gray Birch (London, 1892), p. xiii. Such a wall was characteristic only of British churches. See G. Baldwin Brown, The Arts in Early England (London, 1926), I, 182.

[42] Barbara C. Turner, The Churches of Medieval Winchester (Winchester, 1957), p. 421.

[43] "Laws of Athelstan," EHD, p. 384.

[44] R. N. Quirk, "Winchester Cathedral in the Tenth Century," Archaeological Journal, CXIV (1957), 29.

[45] Cornelius Walford, "The History of Gilds," The Antiquarian Magazine and Bibliographer, II (1882), 300.

[46] "Liber Winton," Domesday Book, seu Libri Censualis, Willelmi Primi Regis Angliae, Addimento ex Codic. Antiquiss. Great Britain Public Records Commission, IV (1816), 529-562.

[47] "Liber Winton," p. 533.

[48] D. P. Kirby, The Making of Early England (New York, 1967), p. 257. See also J. S. Furley, The Ancient Usages of the City of Winchester (Oxford, 1927).

[49] Alfred C. Piper, "The Parchment Making Industry in Winchester and Hampshire," Library, 3rd ser., X (1919), 65-68.

[50] Whitelock, p. 129.

[51] Eric John, The Popes (New York, 1954), passim.

[52] G. G. Perry, A History of the English Church, 5th ed. (London, 1890), I, 125.

[53] Daniel Rock, The Church of Our Fathers as Seen in St. Osmund's Rite for the Cathedral of Salisbury, ed. G. W. Hart and W. H. Frere (London, 1905), I, 141-142.

[54] Translated in Robert S. Lopez, The Tenth Century: How Dark the Dark Ages? (New York, 1959), p. 29.

[55] John Godfrey, The Church in Anglo-Saxon England (Cambridge, 1962), p. 479; Kathleen Edwards, The English Secular Cathedrals in the Middle Ages (Manchester, 1967), p. 10, n. 1.

[56] J. R. H. Moorman, A History of the Church in England, 2nd ed. (London, 1967), p. 50.

[57] The exact number of churches cannot be determined. By 1282 there were between forty-seven and sixty-two churches in Winchester. See The History and Antiquites of Winchester (Winchester, 1773), II, passim.

[58] *A History of Hampshire and the Isle of Wight,* II, 9.

[59] Whitelock, p. 166.

[60] *EHD,* p. 380.

[61] "Episcopus," *Die Gesetze der Angelsachsen,* ed. Felix Liebermann (Halle, 1903), I, 477-479.

[62] The altercation between seculars and regulars was essentially one between the nobility on one hand and a group comprised of initiates from all classes on the other.

[63] *Chronicon Monasterii de Abingdon,* ed. Joseph Stevenson. Rerum Britannicarum Medii Aevi Scriptores, No. 2 (London, 1858), I, 358-366.

[64] *EHD,* pp. 381-387.

[65] "Vita Odonis," *Anglia Sacra,* ed. Henry Wharton (London, 1691), pp. 79ff; *The Historians of the Church of York and Its Archbishops,* ed. James Raine (London, 1879), I, 400-410.

[66] D. J. V. Fisher, "The Anti-Monastic Reaction in the Reign of Edward the Martyr," *Cambridge Historical Journal,* X (1952), 264.

[67] Perry, I, 108-109.

CHAPTER II

THE MONASTIC REVIVAL

The simple entry in the <u>Anglo-Saxon Chronicle</u> for the year 964, "in this year the canons were expelled from the Old Minster,"[1] suggests little of the violence, recriminations, and ramifications, especially in the artistic realm, that resulted from this bold deed which signalled the active beginning of the Monastic Revival. Contemporary but contradictory accounts of the reform movement abound, but from the confusion, one important conclusion is undeniable: with the king's aid, Ethelwold, Dunstan, and Oswald initiated an undertaking which made English monasticism

> for the first time, definitely educational in its aim and national in its scope; it carried on and amplified the tradition of Alfred by translating patristic works into English and by continuing the Old English <u>Chronicle</u>; and it embraced forms of literature and music and the minor fine arts such as illumination, carving, and metal-work."[2]

A detailed account of the relationship of religious drama to the Monastic Revival has been lacking, but such connections become clearer upon examination of the lives of the executors of the Monastic Revival and the results of their work. In the process John Britton's feeling of being "constantly perplexed in the mazes of fable, tradition and probable narration; and [I] feel extreme difficulty in discriminating the one from the other, and rendering our account rational, satisfactory, and authentic"[3] is understandable.

Dunstan, Abbot and Bishop

In 1874 William Stubbs assessed Dunstan's work in the reform movement as that of a sentitious adviser: "Ethelwold was the moving spirit, Oswald tempered zeal with discretion, Dunstan's hand may be credited with such little moderation and practical wisdom as can be traced."[4] Stubbs's rabid anti-clericalism, especially his animus toward Ethelwold, influenced most writers on the Monastic Revival until Eric John in 1960 fairly demonstrated Ethelwold's prudent leadership.[5] Acceptance of either man, however, as the ultimate leader of the movement depends on historical perspective. Dunstan's deeds are important, so vital that Ethelwold's attainments might have been impossible without him, and the fact that historians, both medieval and modern, have seen in Dunstan the subject of several books makes it necessary to recount his adventures as a means of understanding the Monastic Revival. The task is somewhat ameliorated by the wealth of contemporary and modern biographies: <u>The Life of St. Dunstan</u> (c. 1000) by an anonymous author called B;[6] <u>The Life of St. Dunstan</u> (c. 1011) by Adelard, a monk of St. Peter's Abbey, Ghent; <u>The Life of St. Dunstan</u> (c. 1080/90) by Osbern, Precentor of Christchurch, Canterbury; [8] The Life of St. Dunstan (early twelfth century) by Eadmer, Precentor of Christchurch, Canterbury; [9] The Life of St. Dunstan (after 1120) by William of Malmesbury; [10] Memorials of St. Dunstan (1874) by William Stubbs; [11] and The Times of St. Dunstan (1923) by J. Armitage Robinson. [12] Scholarship is indebted to Eleanor S. Duckett for her methodical study, Saint Dunstan of Canterbury (1955); [13] indeed, the works of B and Duckett are the most reliable sources, but the others add some interesting details.

Dunstan was born in 909[14] to wealthy parents in a Somerset village near Glastonbury Abbey, which from an early date was associated by legend with Joseph of Arimathea, King Arthur, and St. Patrick, who was buried there. The unseemly conduct of the secular canons who inhabited the abbey church, which was neglected and in disrepair, did not dim young Dunstan's reverence of the place. As a youth Dunstan lived with the inmates of Glastonbury, and they, as well as frequent Irish pilgrims, were Dunstan's teachers. He studied the Bible, scriptural interpretation, Latin, mathematics, saints' lives, and the ancient histories of his homeland.

The year 923 was significant for Dunstan because his uncle Athelm, Bishop of Wells, was elevated to the see of Canterbury and invited Dunstan, already devoted to a religious vocation, to live in the archiepiscopal palace at Canterbury. Athelm introduced Dunstan to King Athelstan, whom he had crowned in 924(?); at Athelm's death the next year, Athelstan asked Dunstan to attend him. For the next eight or nine years, then, Dunstan was to be seen frequently at court, where he saw an impressive conflux of alien dignitaries, political intriguers, and counselors of war. Luxuriating in this heady atmosphere, Dunstan developed an interest in tapestries, metal-work, and painting. He read poetry, drew pictures, studied music, and attracted attention because of his aloofness, asceticism, and lack of bellicosity. Dunstan also encountered ecclesiastical courtiers, notably the two Elfheahs, one of whom became Bishop of Wells in 926 and the other who was consecrated Bishop of Winchester in 934. Soon Dunstan's austerity and serious demeanor created enemies who defamed him to the king. Athelstan finally was persuaded that Dunstan practiced the black arts (a capital offense) and banished him from the court, but not before the young man was severely beaten by his opponents.

During this dark period of disfavor, Dunstan passed his days in Glastonbury and Winchester examining his life and future prospects. From Bishop Elfheah, Dunstan perceived that he might be able to maneuver events toward the restoration of observance of the Rule of St. Benedict; Elfheah himself, with a few followers, was trying to lead a regular life, but he was not in a position to engineer a return to monastic purity, nor was the nation then prepared to support such a movement. Elfheah's triumph, though, was convincing Dunstan that he could accomplish such a formidable deed, although the young man's conversion to this principle was gradual. Perhaps the remembrance of his stimulating life at court attracted Dunstan more than Elfheah's seemingly impossi-

36

ble dream, but a crucial illness in 936 prompted him to return to Glastonbury, study the Benedictine Rule, celebrate the rites of the church, and lead into the cenobitic life anyone who would follow. These things he did, while taking every opportunity to visit Winchester for refreshment and counsel with Elfheah, who ordained Dunstan priest soon after Dunstan's momentous decision. On the same day Elfheah made a priest of his nephew Ethelwold.

When Edmund became king, he revoked Dunstan's banishment and summoned the monk to court as a trusted adviser. No sooner had Dunstan reacclimated himself to the regal environment than his enemies resurrected their calumnies. Edmund became the second king to send Dunstan from his presence, but before Dunstan could complete arrangements to journey to eastern Europe with some foreign envoys, a miraculous delivery from a riding accident persuaded the king to forgive Dunstan and to create him Abbot of Glastonbury.

In addition to study, contemplation, and prayer, Dunstan filled his days with superintending the physical enlargement of his buildings at Glastonbury, the nature of which is revealed by twentieth-century excavations.[15] He dedicated the next thirteen years to acquiring books and teaching his brethren the monastic way of life as he understood it. His busy days were interrupted by a sad task in 946, the entombment of King Edmund in the abbey church of Glastonbury.

Edred's reign was troubled by sickness and Viking wars but buttressed by Dunstan's love and concern. Devoted to his duties as Abbot of Glastonbury, Dunstan refused the bishoprics of Winchester in 951 and Crediton in 953. As trusted adviser of the king, Dunstan kept part of the royal treasury at Glastonbury. Edred finally succumbed to ill health in 955 and was buried by Dunstan in the Old Minster, Winchester.

Edwig's regime was distinguished by his hostility toward Dunstan. Some of the difficulty was caused by Dunstan's admonitory reaction to Edwig's liaison with a calculating woman called Elgifu and her ambitious mother Ethelgifu. At Edwig's coronation feast, Dunstan bodily forced the young king to entertain his guests rather than amuse himself privately with this woman whose kinship precluded an honorable marriage.

As a result of this incident -- doubtless the whisperers were still vicious too -- Dunstan left England in 956, perhaps of his own volition, probably in exile. In assessing Dunstan's importance at this point in his life, Duckett overstates his accomplishments when she claims that the Monastic Revival was the direct result of "the new and original impulse given by Elfheah at Winchester and furthered by Dunstan at Glastonbury; that given by Berno and Odo at Cluny and transmitted to Fleury; that given by John of Gorze to the Netherlands, in the mediaeval duchy of Lotharingia."[16] Each of these influences was considerable, but none was as indispensable as the person of Ethelwold himself.

A few words about Lotharingian monasticism are necessary because Dunstan passed his exile in this region. A growing sense of spiritual concern caused Gérard of Brogne to lead a group of committed followers into the practice of the Benedictine Rule in the church of St. Peter and St. Eugenius between 920 and 928, and from there observance of the Rule spread throughout Lotharingia. A monk named John reformed the abbey of Gorze in Lorraine, which, like the Lotharingian houses, was known for bodily austerity in the observance of the Rule. That Dunstan should sojourn in this region is entirely credible because monastic acerbity appealed to him and relations between England and Lotharingia were quite amicable.

Dunstan decided to enter the community of St. Peter's at Ghent, to which the abbey of St. Bavo's was a twin; St. Peter's is sometimes called Blandinium after the height upon which the monastery stood. Gérard had been asked to reform the twin houses around 941, and he dedicated twelve years to purifying the observance there. Beyond the fact that Womar was abbot of a zealous community of about twenty monks, little of Dunstan's stay in Ghent is known, since he is not mentioned in the annals of the monasteries. [17] Doubtless he listened to stories of monastic reformation, political activity, and the intricacies of liturgical tradition. His mind filled with reformative lore, [18] Dunstan returned to England in 957, having been summoned by Edgar to be his counselor in the governance of the north and east of England which he had wrested from the ineffectual Edwig.

The political situation that greeted Dunstan's arrival was amenable to his plans: a new party of nobility committed to strengthening the monarchy through religious revival had emerged in support of Edgar, a king who was only fourteen years old, ardent in the faith, and anxious to see proper Christian values restored. Since Edwig, who had been deposed, still controlled the west of England around Glastonbury, the king's council was undecided about how to employ Dunstan's services; he obviously could not return to his abbey. So it was agreed that Dunstan must become a bishop "above all, in order that he might constantly be at hand to aid the King with his sage and foresighted counsels." [19] Apparently no particular episcopacy was given to Dunstan at his consecration, but later in 957 he was named Bishop of Worcester when that place fell vacant.

When Elfheah of Canterbury died, Edwig appointed the aged Elfsige of Winchester to fill the primatial position, but on his way to Rome to receive the pope's confirmation, the old man died in the wintry Alps. So Brihthelm, formerly Bishop of Wells, was elevated to the see of Canterbury in 959, and Dunstan became Bishop of London as well as of Worcester. The year 959 was significant for other reasons as well: Gérard died in Brogne: Edwig passed away, and Edgar became monarch of Wessex, Mercia, and Northumbria. Believing Brihthelm not to be forcible enough to execute sweeping reforms, Edgar sent him back to his former post at Wells and in 960 appointed Dunstan metropolitan at Canterbury. That very year Dunstan traveled to Rome to receive the pallium from the pope, doubtless visiting reformed houses along the way. Upon his return to England, Dunstan's life was quite different than it had been. It is convenient to leave Dunstan's story at this point and discuss the activities of his associates until the time when their lives became intertwined.

Ethelwold, Bishop of Winchester

Modern writers have been kinder to Ethelwold than were their nineteenth-century predecessors, who saw in the Bishop of Winchester only ruthlessness and guile. The rehabilitation of Ethelwold's reputation is largely the work of Eric John,[20] although others have reached similar conclusions. Known in his day as the "Father of Monks," Ethelwold's adventures inspired only two contemporary biographers and no modern ones: The Life of St. Ethelwold (1005/6)[21] by AElfric seems to be a relatively reliable source which is supplemented by another Life of St. Ethelwold (late tenth- or early eleventh-century)[22] by Wulfstan. AElfric's account is more credible since he was a pupil of Ethelwold and an observer of the events he discusses.[23]

Born in Winchester during the reign of Edward the Elder (908?) of well-to-do parents and given a suitable education, Ethelwold entered the household of Athelstan as a courtier (comitatus). There he learned much about political manipulation, a skill which he later practiced with consummate ease. At Athelstan's urging he took holy orders and in time was ordained to the priesthood by his uncle Elfheah at the same time as Dunstan, who was probably a year his junior. The goodly Bishop of Winchester is said to have predicted that both would become bishops and that one of the young priests would succeed him as Bishop of Winchester.[24] Ethelwold remained under Elfheah's tutelage, doubtless receiving the same sort of inspiration that Elfheah had given to Dunstan concerning the need for monastic reform. Leaving Winchester, Ethelwold enlisted as a monk at Glastonbury under Abbot Dunstan; he assumed there the office of dean, a disciplinary overseer. By his holiness, humility, and erudition, Ethelwold impressed his fellow monks. The chronicles suggest that when these mild tactics failed to elicit proper monastic conduct, Ethelwold knew how to apply godly force as well.

After a time at Glastonbury, Ethelwold felt that he had exhausted the possibilities of the place (which was not yet strictly Benedictine) and voiced his intention of going abroad to study the reformed monasteries in France and Flanders; he was particularly interested in Fleury-on-the-Loire, a sisterhouse of Cluny, the great center of monastic reformation. For some unknown reasons (possibly because the king could not afford to lose the services of such a bright young man), Edred allowed his mother to persuade him to prevent Ethelwold's passage.[25] As compensation for thwarting Ethelwold's wishes, Edred gave him the derelict abbey at Abingdon at which to implement his concept of proper monastic life.

In that year of 946(?) Abingdon was in a piteous, debilitated state. The buildings were in shambles, and most of the monastery's lands had been absorbed by the king. Having imported some brethren from Glastonbury[26] (possibly seculars), who were willing to submit to the Rule as interpreted by Ethelwold, he then approached the king about reconstituting the monastery's physical endowment. All the monk' lands were returned, and the royal family spent lavishly in restoring the buildings and ceremonial treasures.[27] King Edred supported the project by his presence as well as by his purse, as did Edwig. Ethelwold himself gave the abbey church a great golden chalice, three silver and gold crosses of superb craftmanship, thuribles, vessels, lavers, candelabra cast from molten silver, three hundred books with silver covers [author's italics], and an organ.[28] Ethelwold's love of organs was chronic, as was Dunstan's, and their appreciation of music was indulged by the casting of bells, which they donated to the abbey.[29] The Chronicle of Abingdon also describes a golden wheel which was used only on special holy days to excite the awesome worship of the monastic congregation.[30] The value of the golden wheel notwithstanding, the gift of the three hundrd books exceeds the bounds of magnanimity even of a rich man.

Abbot Ethelwold sublimated his desire to travel abroad by sending Osgar to Fleury to absorb and report to Ethelwold what he learned of the Benedictine observance in that great house. Osgar's return early in the reign of Edgar resulted in the establishment of the Rule of St. Benedict at Abingdon, the first regular monastic house in tenth-century England. Ethelwold ruled his community with wisdom and compassion but did not tolerate foolishness or lack of seriousness. Only his translation to the bishopric of Winchester brought his happy abbacy to a close. One of his first acts as bishop was the expulsion of the clerks from the Old Minster, but the activities of Oswald must be mentioned before that historic scene at Winchester is described.

Oswald, Bishop of Worcester

In some ways Oswald's connections and preparation caused him to be more suited to mounting a revolution than were his two episcopal colleagues. Ethelwold and Dunstan, both of upper-class southern families, claimed Elfheah of Winchester as mentor; Oswald's preceptor was Oda, onetime Bishop of Ramsbury and later Archbishop of Canterbury. Oda has already appeared in these pages as the primary forerunner of the Monastic Revival, and with his nephew Oswald he shared Danish descent. Details of Oswald's activities have come down in the form of a Life of St. Oswald (early eleventh century)[31] by an anonymous author who might have been Byrtferth, a monk of Ramsey, and another Life of St. Oswald (early twelfth century)[32] by Eadmer, Precentor of Christchurch, Canterbury. J. A. Robinson's little book St. Oswald and the Church of Worcester (1919)[33] is helpful in reconciling the contemporary lives with the annals of the various monasteries; some of Robinson's misconceptions are pointed out in another context.

His parents having converted to Christianity from paganism and established themselves as persons of quality in the Danelaw (the area of England settled by the Vikings), Oswald was baptized a Christian and placed in the household of his uncle Oda to be educated. Oda commissioned Frithegode, a learned monk and mathematician, to be Oswald's teacher, and from that egregious monk, Oswald received an appreciation of the lore and literature of the church. As Oswald grew older and demonstrated a fondness for holy things, Oda provided money to purchase for Oswald a monastery in Winchester for his own religious observances. Naturally the great Old and New Minsters were not purchasable in this way, but it was easy enough to obtain one of the smaller churches in the royal city, since every church in England had a proprietor--the king, a bishop, or some member of the earl class. [34] Oswald then assumed the direction of his group of seculars, [35] but after accepting Oda's concept of a truly monastic clergy, Oswald grew discontented with the materialistic existence of his priests. He then petitioned his uncle to send him to the continent to experience the reform movement firsthand; Oda was pleased to send him to Fleury, the community which had given Oda his monastic habit. Since Oswald took a gift to each of the twelve brethren and Abbot Wulfald of Fleury, he was received enthusiastically, and soon afterward he settled into the life of a Benedictine monk. Oswald found life in Fleury far different from that of Winchester where the seculars "kept an excellent table, were tailored to the utmost in the quality and cut of their cloaks and cassocks, and lived in houses of their own."[36]

While applying himself to his studies, Oswald advanced through the diaconate and the priesthood, memorized all the celebrations and rites so he would be able to share them in England. As he officiated at the Divine Office, the monks marvelled at the beauty and mellifluence of his voice. His companions in the great house presumably were congenial: he probably met there an oblate named Abbo, who would one day be his colleague in England; his friend Germanus of Winchester and Ethelwold's emissary Osgar were also at Fleury at that time.

Oswald's halcyon days were interrupted in 959 when he received word that Oda was dying and wished him to return home immediately, but he arrived too late to comfort his beloved uncle. Oswald's bereavement was somewhat vitiated by a kind offer by his Danish kinsman Osketel, Archbishop of York, to travel to Rome with him. Germanus joined the party, which doubtless sojourned at reformed monasteries along the way, and when Osketel returned to York, Oswald and Germanus stayed behind at Fleury.

Archbishop Osketel was desirous of making some important changes in his diocese and wrote Oswald to come to York to help him implement his plans. It was in the capacity of aide to Osketel that Oswald attracted the attention of Dunstan, who, when he was elevated to Canterbury, had Oswald appointed Bishop of Worcester in his stead.

Three bishops trained in various ways and dedicated to the Benedictine Rule had now appeared and bided their time: the only ingredient lacking was a king who would support their schemes. Such a monarch was Edgar. His remarkable compliance is emphasized by comparing his services to the monks with those of his predecessors.

The Tenth-Century Monks and Their Kings

The appointment of Elfheah as Bishop of Winchester in 934 presaged the Monastic Revival. He assumed the monastic life when he accepted his bishop's miter, and he impregnated the minds of both Ethelwold and Dunstan with devotion to the Benedicitine Rule. A monk who preached monastic reform was thus on the chief West Saxon episcopal throne. Why, it might be asked, was Elfheah not allowed to reform Glastonbury, the most conspicuous West Saxon monastery? The overriding answer must be that King Athelstan would not allow him such latitude. The circumstances surrounding Edmund's gift of Glastonbury to Dunstan have been detailed, but it cannot be said that Edmund was a particular friend of monasticism, especially after he gave the lands of Bath Abbey to a group of displaced seculars fleeing the reforms of Gérard of Brogne. Obviously Edmund did not espouse reform.

Edred encouraged Dunstan's work at Glastonbury but did not contribute to the spread of the new doctrines. When Edwig succeeded to the throne, Dunstan's work was interrupted by his exile. So before the reign of Edgar, the only monastic reformers in important positions were Archbishop Oda and Abbot Dunstan. Elfheah was powerless in Winchester, while Ethelwold was abbot only of a small, partially-reformed house, and Oswald was still a student at Fleury. When Edwig was dispossessed of all his kingdom except Wessex, the monastic party (including Dunstan and like-minded nobles) stood squarely behind Edgar. Oda remained with Edwig but ventured to consecrate Dunstan Bishop of Worcester and London despite the king. When Oswald returned from France and found his uncle dead, his first move was to travel north, casting his lot with Edgar en route to Osketel in York. It is not surprising that when Edgar reunited the kingdom at Edwig's death, the monks came to power, Ethelwold's remaining faithful to Edwig notwithstanding. Lest it be wondered why Ethelwold's allegiance to Edwig did not alienate Edgar, it should be mentioned that Edgar had been reared by monks and his tutor had been Ethelwold, who guided and protected Edgar during the tumultuous months of Edwig's reign. In fact, Ethelwold emerged as Edgar's principal counselor. [37]

Ethelwold at Winchester

Ethelwold was consecrated Bishop of Winchester on 29 November 963. What activities filled his initial weeks in office cannot be discovered by examining the contemporary records. In all likelihood he held private conversations with and delivered public exhortations to the loose-living secular canons then occupying both minsters at Winchester; there were probably frequent councils including members of both parties, perhaps with the king himself as arbitrator. It has been popular to characterize Ethelwold as ruthless, overly zealous, and callous; that such an opinion requires revision is shown by his delay in carrying out reforms in his own diocese. Surely he was not idle during the days between 29 November 963 and 20 February 964, the date of his dramatic and forcible expulsion of the clerks from the Old Minster.

On that day, accompanied by Osgar, several other monks from Abingdon, and, representing the king, thegn Wulfstan of Dalham, Bishop Ethelwold went to the doors of the conventual church (the Old Minster) on the first Sunday of Lent. The sound of the antiphon for Communion,

> Serve the Lord with fear,
> and rejoice unto Him with reverence;
> Take hold upon discipline,
> lest ye perish from the right way

greeted the reformers, most of whom had monastic cowls in their hands. Osgar then voiced the sentiment of the entire band, "Why should we tarry outside? Let us go in, and, walking in the way of right, let us serve with fear and joy our Lord God...."[38] According to AElfric, the whole group decided to be bold, thus taking the initiative from Osgar.[39] In either case, the righteous bishop and his retinue advanced toward the choir, and Ethelwold ordered the monks to throw the cowls upon the floor. "Do you know," demanded Ethelwold, "what you have been chanting?" The clerks answered that they knew. Ethelwold then delivered his peroration: "Then if it is good to serve the Lord with fear and to rejoice in Him with reverence, take hold now upon discipline -- and discipline -- means this monk's habit -- lest you do perish, as you were singing, from the right way!" Somewhat stunned by this ultimatum, the clerks said that they would do as Ethelwold commanded on the next day, cras. Not to be put off, the bishop, seconded by Wulfstan, firmly stated: "Now understand me. No longer will I listen to this cras cras cawing about 'tomorrow'! Either you take hold of discipline here and now, or here and now you leave your stalls in this Cathedral Church!"[40] Rather than face such a ruinous course, the seculars fled from the church, but after a while, three returned agreeing to accept the Rule: Eadsige, Wulsige, and Wilstan the priest. The reformation of the Old Minster proceeded rather smoothly thereafter despite the abortive attempt of the seculars to poison Ethelwold. The New Minster and the Nunnaminster next received the attention of the new bishop.

In 965 the New Minster was just over sixty years old and had never been the home of monks, so the expulsion of the clerks there was not greeted with great astonishment. Ethelwold's will prevailed in the New Minster in 965, and a body of young and old monks came from Abingdon to form a nucleus of regulars there under the abbacy of Athelgar, one of Ethelwold's former pupils. The presence within the monastic precincts of the Nunnaminster allowed the bishop to demonstrate early that the orders of religious women were not to be spared his corrective measures; he instituted new rules and appointed Ethelthryth abbess over the Nunnaminster with its chapel dedicated to the Virgin.

Now Ethelwold was in a position to "spread his wings," as AElfric says,[41] and extend his reforms outside Winchester. He appointed his colleague Osgar Abbot of Abingdon and added substantially to the properties of his old community. Burh, formerly called Medeshamestede and later known as Peterborough, was Ethelwold's next settlement (966). He had bought the lands from the king and some nobles. Burh's abbot Ealdwulf later became Bishop of Winchester and Archbishop of York. Seeing the ruins of a convent at Ely, Ethelwold purchased the property from the king and established there in 970 a large community of monks under his former student Brihtnoth.[42] His acquisition of derelict monasteries by no means completed, Ethelwold procured the abbey at Thorney and installed twelve monks under Godeman. In 972-3 he built there a cloister and a church.[43]

Ethelwold's opulent gifts to Abingdon have been catalogued above. Whether these treasures came from Ethelwold's private funds or from grants of the king is uncertain, but it is not surprising that the wealthy abbot spent lavishly upon the foundation of his first monastery. His generosity to Peterborough, whether bestowed as a citizen or as a bishop, indicates that Ethelwold was a patron of the minor arts, well-acquainted with the literature of his age, and disposed to magnificence of religious ritual, an important trait for the creator of religious drama. To the monastery at Peterborough he gave

> a gospel book adorned with silver and 3 crosses likewise decorated with silver, 2 silver candlesticks and 2 covered with gold, and 1 silver censer and 1 made of brass and 1 silver water vessel and 2 silver bells and 4 silver chalices, 4 patens and a silver tube and 6 mass vestments and 4 copes and 1 upper garment and 8 stoles, the same number of napkins and 11 subuculas and 2 epistle vestments and 3 corporals and 3 offering cloths and 19 albs and 4 cloaks and 2 webs of linen for albs and 2 black robes... and 6 wall curtains and 9 seat covers and 10 hanging bells, 7 hand bells and 4 bed covers and 6 horns -- 4 of them decorated -- and 8 silver cups and 2 gilded altar cloths."[44]

This list of vessels and vestments should be compared with the requirements of the Visitation to the Sepulchre as described in the Monastic Agreement; it seems as if Ethelwold took special care that Peterborough would possess the accouterments of the drama. If a tiny house such as Peterborough commanded such opulence, the mind boggles at considering the array of vestments and treasures in Ethelwold's cathedral. The monks' most costly goods were not of gold and silver though. They were of parchment, vellum, ink, and paint--books.

Books were so scare in the tenth century that Ethelwold's gift seems nearly profligate: Bede's commentary on the Gospel of Mark, the Book of Wonders, [45] Exposition of Hebrew Names, Prophecy of Future Events, [46] Augustine's On Academies, a verse Life of St. Felix by Paulinus of Nola, the Synonyms of Isidore of Seville, a Life of Eustace, Abbo of St. Germain's Destruction of Paris, Medicine, On Twelve Abuses, A Sermon on Certain Psalms, A commentary on the Song of Songs, On the Eucharist, a commentary by Martin Capella, Alcimus Avitus, a Book of Differences, Caecilius Cyprian, a Book of Beasts, and On Greek letters. [47] Ethelwold must have been particularly impressed by the Gospel of Mark, for when he dramatized the Visitation to the Sepulchre, he utilized only one angel (as in Mark and Matthew); Luke and John describe two heavenly guardians of the tomb. Peterborough's library was of incalculable worth and shows a great deal of perspicacity on the part of the donor.

AElfric's description of Ethelwold's activities at this time has been used to detract from his character, but in an age of extremes, his behavior does not seem to deserve censure:

> And Ethelwold went round the individual monasteries, establishing good usages by admonishing the obedient and correcting the foolish with rods. He was terrible as a lion to the disobedient or undisciplined, but gentler than a dove to the gentle and humble. He was a father of monks and nuns, a comforter of widows and a restorer of the poor, a defender of churches, a corrector of those going astray, for he performed more by his work than we can relate in words. [48]

This passage suggests that as a monastic bishop, Ethelwold tended to secular responsibilities and did not sequester himself within his own monastery. These words of AElfric, even if suspiciously effusive, are indicative of the kind of loyalty the energetic bishop could command. Ethelwold's last days were spent "as a kind of visitor-general for the king, going from one monastery to another and insisting on strict obedience to the Benedictine Rule."[49]

The Reformation under Oswald

While Ethelwold proceeded with monastic reformation in his vigorous way, so post-Conquest traditions say,[50] Oswald, consecrated Bishop of Worcester in 961, achieved similar results in a drastically different manner. Whereas the Bishop of Winchester expelled clerks through the exercise of force, his counterpart in Worcester established Benedictinism through utilizing holy guile, winning converts to monasticism through patience and education. Eric John, who has been so instructive about this complex period, has demonstrated that there was very little difference in the methods of the episcopal reformers.[51]

The tiny cathedral church at Worcester, dedicated to St. Peter and managed by seculars, was unable to accommodate the throngs which convened to hear the magnificent voice of their new bishop. Although Oswald preached out-of-doors to his flock, the need to construct a new, more spacious cathedral soon became evident. The new church, St. Mary's, sprang up very quickly owing to the great numbers of people who assisted in the building. For some reason, probably because both churches were dear to him, Oswald considered both St. Peter's and St. Mary's his cathedral churches. Thus far there is little disagreement among the ancient sources.

Dunstan's tenure as Bishop of Worcester had been too short to initiate Benedictinism in that diocese which probably never had been monastic; the task was left to Oswald, and discerning how he actually instituted observance of the Rule in Worcester comprises the gravest critical problem relative to Oswald's ministry. Florence of Worcester, in his entry for 969, claims that Oswald himself admitted to expelling the clerks from Worcester and substituting monks. [52] A local lawsuit corroborates the deed, [53] although some aspects of the testimony are suspicious. Another source, the Altitonantis charter CS 1135, declares:

> Whence now the monastery, which the aforesaid Bishop Oswald has endowed in the episcopal see of Worcester in honour of Mary, the holy Mother of God, and had granted to religious monks serving God -- the debased, degraded, lascivious clerks having been eliminated, with my consent and favour. I [Edgar] confirm [the monastery] to these religious monks by my royal authority. With the counsel and agreement of my ealdormen and my magnates, I grant and confirm [the monastery] so that in future the clerks shall have no right or title for reclaiming anything there, at least those who prefer to stick to their ways, to the detriment of their order and the loss of their prebends, rather than serve God chastely and canonically. Therefore everything belonging to that church that the clerks formerly possessed with the church, either spiritual or secular, movable or immovable, I hand over the these servants of God, the monks, by my royal munificence, to hold from this day forward for ever. [54]

Thus, from these purely Worcester sources one deduces that at some time between 963 and 966, Oswald expelled the seculars from St. Mary's, the new monastic buildings of which were not completed until 984, and instituted another monastic cathedral in England. The Rule of St. Benedict, as practiced at Fleury, was established, but a far-reaching program of education was needed in Oswald's diocese.

He recalled Germanus from Fleury and put him in charge of training the new converts to monasticism; soon Oswald transferred twelve brothers under Germanus to the monastery at Westbury-on-Trym just outside Bristol. The arrival of new oblates strained the capacity of Westbury, so Oswald was forced to seek a more commodious convent. Having taken counsel with his brother-bishops and important nobles, Oswald finally put his problem to King Edgar, who offered him the derelicted houses of St. Albans, Ely, and Benfleet, none of which served Oswald's purpose. He did take St. Albans, though, as a subsidiary house around 970 and placed it under the rule of AElfric, a monk of Abingdon, who later as archbishop introduced monks into Canterbury Cathedral in 1000. Before returning to Worcester, Oswald fell into conversation with Ethelwine, ealdorman of East Anglia, and introduced his problem. As a result, Ethelwine donated to the monks his property at Ramsey in Huntingdonshire, a site rich in good soil, clean water, abundant fish and fowl, and isolation. Oswald installed Ethelnoth, superior at Westbury, as monk in charge of preparing the grounds; some time later in 969/70 Germanus and the twelve monks journeyed from Westbury and inhabited the new place. The abbey church was functional the next spring, but it was not until 974 that Oswald, then Archbishop of York as well as Bishop of Worcester, dedicated the complex of buildings to Mary, St. Benedict, and all holy Virgins. Wynsige, who had been trained at Ramsey, returned to direct the exercises of the monks at Worcester Cathedral.

It is difficult to establish the exact number of monasteries reformed by Oswald, since his sphere of influence overlapped Ethelwold's. He probably reconstituted Deerhurst. The Bishop of Worcester assumed control over Winchcombe and brought monks from Ramsey to form a nucleus with Germanus as abbot. Ethelwold and Oswald collaborated in the restoration of Pershore and set over the place a former monk of Glastonbury and Abingdon, Foldberht. The crusading bishops joined forces once again by re-establishing Evesham and appointing another monk named Oswald as abbot; later Frithegar, who had studied with both Dunstan and Ethelwold, became the father of the community. Ethelwold, Oswald, and Dunstan may have worked together through their mutual friend Thurketel in the endowment of Crowland some time after 971. How many monasteries actually benefited from Oswald's ministrations cannot be deduced accurately, but the number must be considerable.

As bishops, Ethelwold and Oswald could not be impervious to the needs of the secular clerks who were charged with maintaining the spiritual welfare of the masses. They worked tirelessly in training priests, visiting the poor and needy, and preaching in the parish churches. Oswald was elevated to the Archbishopric of York in 971/72. His remaining years were characterized by discernment, unrelenting activity on the part of the church, and sage counsel both in large and small affairs. Meanwhile Dunstan was furthering the Monastic Revival in his new role as Archbishop of Canterbury.

Dunstan at Canterbury

Dunstan journeyed to Rome to receive the pallium in 960. After visiting the monastery of St. Bertin, Dunstan returned to his archiepiscopal cathedral, recently redecorated by his predecessor Oda. In Canterbury Dunstan tried to live as a Benedictine monk, but he did not forcibly install regulars in the cathedral church, a deed which was not accomplished until 1000. In all probability, though, Dunstan's example attracted others to the Benedictine way of life, and he encouraged them to live regularly at Canterbury. An extremely literate man, Dunstan studied diligently in order better to instruct his ministers and spent hours in the scriptorium correcting errors in the beautiful manuscripts. He was not divorced wholly from the monastic life because St. Augustine's Abbey, dedicated to SS. Peter and Paul, was still actively regular. Dunstan's monastic zeal was doubtless served by his activities in behalf of the monasteries outside Canterbury. While still Bishop of London, he installed twelve monks in the small church of St. Peter's, Westminster, but as archbishop, his deeds included bestowing expensive gifts upon Glastonbury, encouraging the re-establishment of monkish discipline at King Alfred's royal abbeys at Athelney and Muchelney, and affirming the monastic character of the foundation at Bath. It will be remembered that King Edmund had given the convent at Bath to refugee seculars fleeing the reformers of Lotharingia. Elfheah II, later Bishop of Winchester and Archbishop of Canterbury, had left Deerhurst seeking a stricter life, and he found it at Bath. Dunstan, perhaps, was the cause of the change in the character of that house. Dunstan also sent monks to Malmesbury, but in all these deeds, his hand is disguised. Exactly what were his contributions to any monastery is impossible to say.

As Duckett points out,[55] Dunstan's services to the Benedictine ideal are not to be underrated. He established the first semi-regular tenth-century monastery in the country at Glastonbury; he contributed a firsthand knowledge of foreign monastic practices; his mouth was always near the king's ear encouraging his support of the reform; and he appointed men who would execute the grand scheme of the Monastic Revival.

As primate, Dunstan travelled widely throughout the country superintending the ministry to the laity and protecting the privileges of the church. As archbishop, he participated in the legislation that enabled the English and the Danes to live together peacefully; Dunstan served in the hundred courts and as judicial adviser to the king. Furthermore, Dunstan drew together the various foreign practices and devised a coronation rite for Edgar, the earliest such English ceremonial, which symbolically strengthened the union between church and state.[56] Dunstan was the elder statesman of the Monastic Revival; if his actual deeds in behalf of the movement are not readily discernible, nevertheless his influence permeates nearly every deed committed by the monks.

The Demise of the King and the Bishops

The events that comprised the first stage of the Monastic Revival -- that is, until 975, the year of Edgar's death -- have been treated. These acts in themselves did not lead to the creation of liturgical music-drama. The results of these exploits, on the other hand, include the composition of the Winchester

Easter play. A description of the events that followed Edgar's demise must precede the narration of those factors.

The passing of the king nearly precipitated a civil war. Edgar left two sons, Edward and Ethelred, by two wives. Dunstan supported the claims of Edward, while the Queen Mother pressed for the coronation of her son, Ethelred, the younger. The rest of the nation chose sides for the forthcoming struggle. The lines were not so clearly drawn as one might suppose at first glance, for there was the matter of the monks to be considered as well. The Monastic Revival strengthened the hold of the king over his nobles, a circumstance that has always been resisted by the hereditary upper classes. Under Edgar, the church inherited lands controlled for generations by the earl class; heirs were disappointed as family fortunes were divided in favor of the monasteries. The monks themselves had become powerful landlords who threatened the envious nobles' commercial rights and judicial invulnerability. Predictably, secular priests, deprived of comfortable livings, hated the monks, who were also deprecated by the commoners who had lost property through the re-establishment of monasteries, such as those in Winchester. Finally, the upper classes resented the monks' recruitment of oblates from all strata of society as an affront to their dignity; the seculars mostly were aristocratic. All in all, it was an exceedingly combustible situation.

Ethelwine, who had given Ramsey to Oswald, repeatedly harrassed Ely, and Elfhere, ealdorman of Mercia, drove monks out of several Mercian monasteries. He expelled the monks from Evesham and caused Germanus to flee from Winchcombe to Fleury and from there to Ramsey. Deerhurst was destroyed at this time.

The succession was resolved finally, probably due to Dunstan's statecraft, in favor of Edward, who was crowned by Oswald and Dunstan in 975 and who died quite mysteriously in 978. The two archbishops crowned Ethelred that same year. One of the chronicles states that in the coronation year, "a cloud red as blood and shot with fire was often seen at midnight,"[57] a fitting augury of Ethelred's reign (978-1016). Dunstan tried to influence the king's actions in support of the monks and was largely successful until the Northmen began their raids anew in 980.

Increasingly Dunstan conserved his waning energy for religious affairs alone, but he appeared in the procession honoring the consecration of the new cathedral in Winchester in 980. Ethelwold's church was such a testament to monastic dedication that a reconciliation among the various factions seemed possible, but the Vikings soon occupied the waking hours of all contenders. Ethelwold died in 984, and Dunstan appointed Elfheah II, a monk of Bath, as Bishop of Winchester. Dunstan died in 988, and Oswald departed this life four years later. Some progress in the civilized arts was made after Edgar's death, but the anticipated glories of the Monastic Revival were dispelled by a new period of war and horror.

Notes

[1]ASC, anno 964.

[2]David Knowles, "The Cultural Influence of English Mediaeval Monasticism," Cambridge Historical Journal, VII (1941-3), 150.

[3]John Britton, The History and Antiquities of the See and Cathedral Church of Winchester.... (London, 1817), pp. 9-10.

[4]William Stubbs, "Memorials of St. Dunstan," Historical Introductions to the Rolls Series, ed. Arthur Hassall (London, 1902), p. 18.

[5]Eric John, "The Sources of the English Monastic Reformation: A Comment," Revue Bénédictine, LXX (1960), 197-203.

[6]"Vita Sancti Dunstani auctore B," Memorials of St. Dunstan, ed. William Stubbs. Rerum Britannicarum Medii Aevi Scriptores, No. 63 (London, 1874), 3ff. Extracts are translated in Whitelock, EHD, pp. 826-831.

[7]"Vita Sancti Dunstani auctore Adelardo," Memorials of St. Dunstan, 53ff.

[8]"Vita Sancti Dunstani auctore Osberno," Memorials of St. Dunstan, 69ff.

[9]"Vita Sancti Dunstani auctore Eadmero," Memorials of St. Dunstan, 162ff.

[10]"Vita Sancti Dunstani auctore Willelmi Malmesburiensis," Memorials of St. Dunstan, 250ff.

[11]Stubbs, Historical Introductions, 1ff.

[12]J. A. Robinson, The Times of St. Dunstan (London, 1922).

[13]Eleanor S. Duckett, Saint Dunstan of Canterbury (London, 1955).

[14]The year of Dunstan's birth has been disputed. In "Annales Anglo-Saxonici breves (925-1202)," Ungedruckte Anglo-Normannische Geschichtsquellen, ed. Felix Liebermann (Strassburg, 1879), p. 3, his birthdate is given as 925: "On þison, geare waes sancte Dunstan geboren. and he leofode. LXIII geare and on þam LXIIII he forþ ferde XIIII kl. Jun." Modern scholars, however, have accepted 909 as the correct year.

[15]J. Williamson, Glastonbury Abbey: Its History and Ruins (Wells, 1862). See also C. A. Ralegh Radford, "Excavations at Glastonbury Abbey," Antiquity, XXV (1951), 213; XXVII (1953), 41; XXIX (1955), 33-34; XXXI (1957), 171.

[16]Duckett, St. Dunstan, p. 59.

[17]Arnold Fayen, ed., Liber Traditionum S. Petri Blandensis (Ghent, 1906); "Les Annales Blandensis," Les Annales de Saint-Pierre de Gand et de Saint-Amand, ed. Philip Grierson (Bruxelles, 1937), 1-73; "Annales Sancti Bavonis Gandensis anonymo auctore," Recueil des Chroniques de Flandre, ed. J.-J. de Smet (Bruxelles, 1837), I, 437-588.

[18]H. Dauphin, "Le Renouveau monastique en Angleterre au Xe siècle et ses rapports avec la reforme de saint Gérard de Brogne," Revue Bénédictine, LXX (1960), 177-196.

[19]Stubbs, Historical Introductions, p. 36.

[20]Eric John, "Sources," passim.

[21]"Vita S. AEthelwoldi episcopi Wintoniensis auctore AElfrico," Chronicon Monasterii de Abingdon, ed. Joseph Stevenson. Rerum Britannicarum Medii Aevi Scriptores, No. 2 (London, 1858), II, 253-266. Translated in EHD, pp. 831-839. Also see Michael Winterbottom, "Three Lives of St. Ethelwold," Medium AEvum, 41 (1972), 191-201.

[22] "Vita Sancti Ethelwoldi auctore Wulstani," Patrologia Latina, ed. J.-P. Migne (Paris, 1899), CXXXVII, 79-114.

[23] For the relation between these lives, see D. J. V. Fisher, "The Early Biographers of St. Ethelwold," English Historical Review, LXVII (1952), 38-91.

[24] AElfric, EHD, p. 833.

[25] AElfric, EHD, p. 833.

[26] According to AElfric (EHD, pp. 833-834), these brethren were Osgar, Foldberht, and Frithegar from Glastonbury; Ordberht from Winchester; and Eadric from London. Later AElfric mentions a monk named Elfstan. Each of these monks later distinguished himself. Osgar became Abbot of Abingdon; Frithegar, Abbot of Evesham; Foldberht, Abbot of Pershore; and Ordberht, Abbot of Chertsy.

[27] Archaeologists have discovered the well-preserved Saxon church under the Norman remains. See Martin Biddle, Gabrielle Lambrick, and J. N. L. Myres, "The Early History of Abingdon, Berks., and Its Abbey," Mediaeval Archaeology, XII (1968), 26-69.

[28] Chronicon Monasterii de Abingdon, I, 344. Ethelwold's gifts to Abingdon included: (1) calicem unum aureum immensi ponderis ob honorem et reverentiam Corporis et Sanguinis Domini Nostri Jhesu Christi; (2) tres cruces admodum decoras ex argento et auro puro; (3) Ornavit etiam ecclesiam textis tam ex argento puro quam ex auro obrizo pariter et lapidus pretiossimis, thuribulis et phialis, pelvibus fusilibus et candelabris ex argento ductilibus, multisque bonis aliis...; (4) fecit argenteam pretio adpretiatem trecentarum librarum, cujus etiam materiam forma exsuperabat artificialis.... II, 278. Organus propriis manibus ipse fecit.

[29] Chronicon Monasterii de Abingdon, I, 345. "Fecit etiam duas campanas propriis manibus...."

[30] Chronicon Monasterii de Abingdon, I, 345. "...fecit ... quandam rotam tintinnabulis plenam ... ad majoris excitationem devotionis...."

[31] "Vita Sancti Oswaldi auctore anonymo," Historians of the Church of York and Its Archbishops, ed. James Raine. Rerum Britannicarum Medii Aevi Scriptores, No. 71 (London, 1879), I, 399-475. Extracts are translated in EHD, pp. 839-843.

[32] "Vita Sancti Oswaldi," Historians of the Church of York, II, 1ff.

[33] St. Oswald and the Church of Worcester (London, 1919).

[34] John Godfrey, The Church in Anglo-Saxon England (Cambridge, 1962), p. 319.

[35] Historians of the Chruch of York, I, 410.

[36] Duckett, St. Dunstan, p. 138.

[37] Eric John, "The King and the Monks in the Tenth-Century Reformation," Orbis Britanniae and Other Studies (Leicester, 1966), p. 160.

[38] Wulstanus, Patrologia Latina, CXXXVII, 91. Osgaro exhortante eos atque dicente: Cur foris moramur? ...ingrediamur, et per viam justitiae gradientes, Domino Deo nostro cum timore et exsultatione famulemur....

[39] EHD, p. 835.

[40] Duckett, St. Dunstan, p. 129.

[41] EHD, p. 836.

[42] *Liber Eliensis*, ed. E.O. Blake. Publications of the Royal Historical Society, Camden 3rd ser., No. 92 (London, 1962), 105, 110.

[43] J.T. Irvine, "Account of the Discovery of Part of the Saxon Abbey Church of Peterborough," Journal of the British Archaeological Association, L (1894) 45-54.

[44] A.J. Robertson, ed., Anglo-Saxon Charters (Cambridge, 1939), p. 72.

[45] This book may be either The Seven Wonders of the World or the Dialogues of Gregory the Great.

[46] Possibly by Julian of Toledo.

[47] Robertson, Anglo-Saxon Charters, p. 72.

[48] EHD, p. 836.

[49] William Hunt, The English Church (London, 1907), I, 354.

[50] In particular, the various lives of Oswald in Historians of the Church of York and William of Malmesbury have contributed to this mistaken notion, and successive scholars have repeated their conclusions.

[51] Eric John, "St. Oswald and the Church of Worcester," Orbis Britanniae and Other Studies (Leicester, 1966), pp. 234-248.

[52] Florentius Wigorniensis, Chronicon ex Chronicis, ed. Benjamin Thorpe (London, 1848), I, 141.

[53] John, "St. Oswald," p. 238.

[54] John, "St. Oswald," p. 236. The actual charter is reproduced in Eric John, Land Tenure in Early England (Leicester, 1960), pp. 162-167.

[55] Duckett, St. Dunstan, p. 93.

[56] J.A. Robinson, "The Coronation Order in the Tenth Century," Journal of Theological Studies, XIX (1917), 71.

[57] Chronicon Monasterii de Abingdon, I, 356.

CHAPTER III

BENEDICTINISM AND THE <u>MONASTIC AGREEMENT</u>

The preceding narration repeatedly suggests the question: What was so compelling about the Rule of St. Benedict that England's monastic reformers insisted upon a rigid observance of it?" A number of cenobitic rules -- among them those of Antony, Pachomius, Basil, Macarius, Aurelian, Cassian, Donatus, Caesarius of Arles, and Columbanus -- were stricter in their demands than Benedict's rule. [1] The special nature, and hence the unique attraction, of Benedict's formulation can be gleaned from the history of the Benedictine order and from the manual itself.

The Rise and Diffusion of Benedictinism

The Rule was devised by Benedict of Nursia (480?-543?), Abbot of Monte Cassino, who

> gave first to central Italy, and then by transmission to the rest of Europe, a form of religious life peculiarly suited to Western temperaments and needs, and he did this by turning away both from the eremetical ideal as it existed in Italy in his day, with its extreme physical austerity, and from the conception of monastic life as a search for perfection now in this monastery and now in that, and by firmly basing his system on a Rule to which absolute obedience was vowed, applied by an abbot to whom that obedience was paid, in a monastery from whose family circle only death could separate the monk who had once joined himself to it. [2]

Drawing upon monastic principles of the past and prognosticating needs of the future, Benedict conceived a rule that is above all a blueprint for developing personal spirituality. "The character which it impressed was one of order, of peace and of benignity, and it became a force of incalculable power not only for sanctification, but also for the lower but indispensable task of civilizing and refining."[3] This fact accounts for the suitability of the Rule of St. Benedict to the needs of England both in the tenth century and in the sixth, when Christianity was first brought to the island kingdom. In the case of the former time, society was in violent upheaval, and in the case of the latter, a barbarous nation had to be evangelized and civilized.

Missionaries dispatched by Pope Gregory the Great landed on the shores of England in 597. Augustine (d. 604), attended by a body of monks from Italy's Coelian monastery, brought with him a concept of monasticism which was a compromise between strict Benedictinism (with its emphasis on personal spirituality and communal living) and Roman basilican monasticism (which stressed the monk's participation in the liturgical exercises of great secular churches). The first English monastery, founded in Canterbury by the Augustinian brothers, was dedicated to SS. Peter and Paul; later ages would know the foundation as St. Augustine's Abbey.

The next half-century witnessed the widespread success of monasticism in England: the Italian persuasion, proceeding from Canterbury, dominated the southern area; in Northumbria, Celtic monasticism was the ideal; and in the midlands, the fen country, and Lincolnshire, a Gallic interpretation of the cenobitic life was introduced by immigrants from Frankish minsters. These varying understandings of the monastic mission had their individual champions, so the story of English monasticism is largely the story of monks in high places.

A brother of Lindisfarne, Wilfrid (634-709/10), returned to England in 658 after several years on the continent and brought with him not only the report of his experiences in Rome and France but also the Rule of St. Benedict, which he introduced into the houses of Ripon and Hexham. Biscop (c. 628-80), a Northumbrian, had shared Wilfrid's travels and sojourned in Rome, where he learned of the Benedictine Rule; his two years as abbot of Canterbury saw the introduction of the Rule into that house. The newly-appointed Archbishop of Canterbury, Theodore the Byzantine (602-90), encouraged observance of the Rule as well.

Benedictinism, albeit a diluted form of it, spread throughout England: Glastonbury, for example, embraced the joint conflux of Celtic and Roman monasticism. Biscop founded the Northumbrian houses of Wearmouth (674) and Jarrow (685), the most celebrated inmate of which was Bede, from whose memory of the monastic life at Jarrow may be deduced that the implementation of the Rule there more closely resembled Benedict's ideal at Monte Cassino than did the practice of any other English house. Biscop's monasticism, on the other hand, was extremely eclectic, so Benedict of Monte Cassino was not the only monkish regulator recognized by this great cleric.

Monasticism flourished to such an extent in England that northern Europe was evangelized by English missionaries under Boniface (680?-755). An English monk named Willibald (700-81) proceeded to Monte Cassino to reform the monastic life there. "Indeed, during the greater part of the eighth century the monasteries of England possessed a life, and exercised an influence, more powerful than those of any monastic bloc in Europe."[2] It was this vitality that Ethelwold and his colleagues sought to recapture in the tenth century.

Simultaneously decay gnawed at the innards of English monasticism. The decline of the English church was quickened by the initial forays of the Northmen, who pillaged Lindisfarne and Jarrow in 793/94. Northern monasticism was obliterated by the Viking attacks of 867-70. While it is true that the southern houses escaped the worst ravages of foreign invasion, their destruction eventuated through internal rot, especially through abandonment of the regular life and implantation of secular clerks in the old minsters. As the English church declined over the eight and ninth centuries, the impetus for the tenth-century revival proceeded from Charlemagne's court.

Charlemagne and the Cluniac Reform

Charles the Great (768-814), seeking to restore the Frankish church to its old dignity, demanded uniformity in monastic observance. Locating what he believed to be the actual holograph of Benedict's Rule, Charlemagne placed copies in all his monasteries and housed the original in his chapel at Aachen. The great king's demands for monastic purity were not realized in his life-time, but after his death monastic reforms were instituted through the collab-oration of Benedict of Aniane (c. 750-821) with Louis the Pious, Charlemagne's successor.

After experimenting with various forms of monastic regulation, Benedict adopted the Rule of St. Benedict in his monastery at Aniane. His success was so great that he was asked to reform other houses as well, and soon the emper-or looked upon him as an arch-abbot responsible for all the abbeys of the Em-pire. In 817 ecclesiastics of the Franks met at Aachen and authorized uniform-ity of observance in all the monasteries; the Rule of St. Benedict was consid-ered normative, even though it was modified by the addition of several innova-tions suggested by Benedict of Aniane: monks were not to be expected to do agricultural work; monks were ordered to educate other regulars solely; addi-tional prayers were appended to those already prescribed by Benedict of Nursia. Thus, these "little chapters" (capitula) of Benedict of Aniane formed the justifi-cation for the singleminded devotion to celebrating the liturgy for an exclusively monastic congregation of the next century.

The enactments of the synod at Aachen represented for Benedict of Aniane the fruits of a long period of collecting various rules, custumals, and historic constitutions of monasticism. His Book of Rules (Codex Regularum) and Agree-ment of Rules (Concordia Regularum) illustrated his contention that the Rule of St. Benedict is preferable to all other systems. Although the Empire soon be-gan to crumble, the work of Benedict of Aniane later affected the monastic re-forms in France, the Low Countries, and England.

Cluny, the great French monastery, was founded in 910 with the intention of adhering to the Rule of St. Benedict as interpreted in the light of recent tra-dition. So that the new foundation might prosper unencumbered by royal control, it was made responsible to the Holy See alone. All the early abbots of Cluny were remarkable men, and under their guidance the abbey prospered both spiritually and physically. Abbots Berno and Odo were asked frequently to bring enlight-ened governance to other houses; consequently, the monastery of Fleury (St. Benedict-on-the-Loire) was reformed around 930, and from there Cluny's effect upon English monasticism can be traced. [5]

In the houses of Fleury, Gorze, and Brogne, the reforms of Benedict of Aniane were known and practiced, so that Cluniac and Flemish monasticism developed that particular essence that was imitated in England: they encompassed "a life of large, well-established communities devoting a very great part of the working hours to liturgical prayer and praise in common, accompanied by elaborate chant and ceremonial; what remained ot the day was given to domestic administration and meditative reading."[6] Thus it happened that a bookish atmosphere conducive to liturgical and artistic experimentation was generated, and because of this sense of freedom, Ethelwold justified artistic experimentation by interpreting the Rule of St. Benedict in the light of Benedict of Aniane's predilections. The Cluniac life, and hence the Winchester life, was essentially liturgical, educational, and artistic, and all these functions were viewed as sanctioned by reformed Benedictinism.

The Rule of St. Benedict

Turning to the Bible as the basis of his system of monastic regulation, Benedict of Nursia states the purpose of the Rule in the prologue: the establishment of a school of God's service,[7] and he makes it quite clear that God's service, though demanding, ought not to be unduly harsh. With great insight, Benedict perceived that his followers would be prone to very human failings; nevertheless, his program was one of personal spiritual development through community living and abbatial rule. This may seem a moot point, but some sixth-century monks frequently moved from house to house without subjecting themselves to any spiritual advisers. Benedict looked upon any activity outside the cloister as particularly undesirable.

Having no idea that he was founding a religious order (in the modern sense of the word), Benedict envisioned each community as autonomous and self-contained. Monks embraced the discipline because they were called to be monks, not in order to execute some other task, such as manuscript illumination or farming, more effectively. The monk's only work was the Work of God, the Opus Dei, which was served by self-discipline, prayer, and work. Both private and communal devotions constituted prayer, as did celebrating the Divine Office in the choir. This work was considered to be so important that Benedict devotes eleven chapters to legislating the nature and number of liturgical ceremonies of the monks. The idea that the monk's major function is liturgical is Benedict's major innovation. The creation of religious drama was merely an extension of this concept.

The Benedictine monk's manual work involves those tasks necessary to maintaining an orderly community; the Rule designates certain responsibilities which are to be rotated among the brethren. Most of the monk's time outside the chapel is spent in reading the Scriptures and the Church Fathers.

The abbot is the sole ruler of the monastery. Benedict admonishes abbots to be humble, prudent, sagacious, and holy, underscoring his caution with the advice that abbots will be responsible at the Last Judgment not only for their own souls but also for those of the monks placed in their care. To settle important matters, the abbot is charged to assemble the community to seek the advice of the young and old without favoritism. Then, when all suggestions have been weighed, the abbot must make the final decision.

The life of the Benedictine is governed by obedience, not only to the will of God but also to the dictates of the abbot. The monk should avoid excessive loquacity; absolute silence is not enjoined, but laughter and frivolity are viewed as harmful to the maintenance of a contemplative atmosphere. The preceding matters comprise the initial seven chapters of the Rule; the following seven stipulate the manner in which the Mass and Canonical Hours are to be celebrated.

In Chapter 20, reverence in all deeds, especially in prayer, is commanded. Large communities have the option of electing deans to assist the abbot in the administration of the monastery's affairs (Chapter 21). Several successive sections regulate the manner in which monks are to sleep and ways in which the brethren are to be punished (Chapters 23-29). The Rule is quite provident toward the discipline of boys in the monastic school. Rather than face excommunication, which is beyond their comprehension, boys are to be whipped and set to fasting (Chapter 30).

The subject of Chapter 31 is the cellerer, the monk in charge of the physical appurtenances of the monastery. All the equipment of the house is to be managed by a delegated monk (Chapter 32), but individual monks may own nothing privately (Chapter 33). Each brother receives from the bounty of the monastery according to his needs and infirmities (Chapter 34). Serving in the kitchen is a responsibility shared by the monks in rotation. Chapter 36 delineates the special care of the ill, and the following section dictates that old men and children should be allowed to eat their meals early.

Since the rule in its entirety must be studied regularly, monks with special gifts should read aloud from Benedict at all meals, during which silence and meditation are urged. The monk's needs for food and drink are satisfied liberally, according to Chapters 49 and 50, but temperance in all things is exhorted. The exact hours for meals are specified in the succeeding chapter.

Benedictines should have no love of idle chatter, and talking at night is banned after the reading of the Church Fathers. In Chapter 43 monks are requested not to be late for Divine Office or meals. Chapters 44-46 describe lapses of discipline and their expiation. Punctuality at the celebration of Divine Office is stressed, as is a certain amount of manual labor. The Rule specifies that monks are either to work with their hands or spend the allotted hours reading holy books. On Sundays monks are to read during all their free time because no other work is permitted.

Chapter 49 deals with Lenten conduct. The traveling monk should celebrate the Hours wherever he might be. No monk within a day's journey from his monastery should partake of food until he returns to his own community.

According to Chapter 52, the oratory of the monastery is to be a place of prayer. Guests are entertained by the abbot and certain designated brethren (Chapter 53); food for travelers is to be provided from a kitchen separate from the one in which the monk's meals are prepared. Monks are not to associate with guests. A monk, says Chapter 54, is to have no contact with the outside world, either through letters, gifts, or tokens. Each monk is given clothes suitable to the climate of his country (Chapter 55). The next section specifies that the abbot's table should be separated from the monks' so he can act as host to guests, in whose honor he may request the presence of a few monks. Artificers are to be allowed to practice their crafts if they can do so humbly (Chapter 57).

The manner in which a monk is created is the material of Chapter 58. The postulant should be made to wait at the door of the convent for several days before being admitted into the guest house. The first stage in becoming a monk is the Novitiate, a period in which the postulant meditates and studies under the guidance of a wise monk who is assigned the task of directing the novice's thinking and evaluating his vocation. After two months' consideration of the difficulties of the monastic calling, the Rule is read to the novice, after which he is asked if he can conform to its demands. If he responds in the affirmative, six months' rigorous training follows. The question of obedience to the Rule is put to him again, and if he maintains his resolution, the novice is guided through four additional months' instruction. Finally, having persevered throughout this grueling test period, the novice is admitted to the brotherhood for life if he still wishes to take his vows.

In the presence of all the brothers assembled in the oratory, the novice promises stability, conversion of life, and obedience; he is asked to sign a contract to that effect. After singing the proper scriptural responses, the newly-elected brother casts himself before the feet of the monks, petitioning their prayers. After this ceremony, he is admitted as an equal member of the community.

Prior to this commitment of body and spirit, the postulant gives all his physical goods to the poor or signs them over to the monastery. At the end of the ordination ceremony, the new monk's clothes are stripped off and replaced by the monastic habit.

The subject of Chapter 59 is parental dedication of infants to the monastery. If noble parents give a child in infancy, they are required to make the vows for the child and to promise that they will never give him any worldly goods. If they choose, the parents may consign their property to the monastery and live off the income; thus the community receives the child's inheritance. Poor people are not required to make gifts when donating their children to the service of God.

Priests are welcomed in the monastery (Chapter 60), but they must obey the Rule and expect no favors. Clerks in minor orders may be accepted also, but they receive no special consideration. Itinerant monks may stop in the monastery if they cause no trouble, but eventually alien monks must secure their abbots' permission to remain in the new monastery. Abbots should select monks from their own communitites to be ordained priests.

The communal hierarchy is established by the abbot on the basis of seniority, exemplary devotion, or some other manifestation of merit (Chapter 63). Normally abbots are elected by the brethren in a given community (Chapter 64). If the chapter of monks believes the abbot requires a deputy, it may elect a prior. The porter's job is to stay near the gate to answer the questions of petitioners.

Brothers who have been sent on a journey must not speak of their travels to the monks who stayed in the cloister (Chapter 67). Monks are not asked to do the impossible, nor should any monk presume to intercede for his brother, nor to strike him, but each should be obedient to the other. Monks should be zealous and charitable toward one another in the exercise of their spirituality.

The final chapter (73) admonishes that perfection in spiritual things is not to be attained by the complete observance of the Rule alone, which is seen only as a minimal expression of the monk's duty to God. The brother must seek in the Bible, the Church Fathers, and other holy books for more exacting requirements for the full life in Christ.

Thus Benedict desired

> to form a community of monks bound to live together until death, under rule, in common life, in the monastery of their profession, as a religious family, leading a life not of marked austerity but devoted to the service of God... the community act of the celebration of the divine office, and in the discipline of a life of ordered daily manual work and religious reading, according to the Rule and under obedience to the abbot. [8]

This is the life that Ethelwold labored to establish in the cloisters of England.

Ethelwold and the English Rule

Several Latin manuscripts of the Rule of St. Benedict have survived from the tenth century, [9] but they were of little value to the monks under Ethelwold's supervision who, with their secular counterparts, [10] were largely unable to read Latin. Faced with the problem of educating prospective teachers, Ethelwold, with the encouragement of Edgar, desired to make the Rule available in English. The resulting translation represented a significant educational advancement, for as Mechthild Gretsch observes, "AEthelwold seems to have endeavoured to make his translation understandable for every member of a monastic house, including those who had very little education; and in so doing he may have preferred understandability attained through repetition and explanation to stylistic elegance. This is why all his additions tend to interpret and explain the Latin original."[11] With respect to the Visitation to the Sepulchre, Ethelwold's strategy was precisely identical. He wished to make the central fact of Christianity, the atoning death and miraculous resurrection of Christ, clear to the same audience which required an English version of the Rule. The use of Latin in the music-drama was not as arcane as its utilization in the Rule because the Latin dialogue was accompanied by pantomimic dramatization. When Ethelwold's English translation of the Rule appeared around 970,[12] Edgar gave Ethelwold the manor of Southbourne, which he donated to his new monastery at Ely.[13]

The Winchester Synod and the Monastic Agreement

By 970 Ethelwold and his associates were advanced in age and saw the necessity of quickening the reformation of the English church in the few years remaining to them. Although Ethelwold's version of the Rule had been disseminated, the problem of monastic diversity remained. While Ethelwold, Dunstan, and Oswald lived, the existence of a somewhat varied observance was no threat to the church. They feared, though, that after their deaths, their successors might fall into error as grave as that of the seculars, error largely occasioned by almost fanatical devotion to the three reformers. New monasteries were founded as sisterhouses of Abingdon, Glastonbury, and Westbury; each new community, consequently, bore the stamp of one of the bishops. "...Dunstan's group, we may assume, had the simplest, most fully English practice; Ethelwold's had elements borrowed from Fleury and Corbie; Oswald's was a pure reproduction of Fleury."[14] To forestall confusion, the reformers decided to place all English monasteries under the direct patronage of the royal family, a move which in the days of Thomas Becket became a decisive factor in the controversy over papal supremacy.

A great synod, therefore, was convened at Winchester at some date between 965 and 975, possibly at Eastertide, to ratify proposals which would regulate monastic observance in the convents where "the Rule of the holy Father Benedict had been accepted with the greatest goodwill."[15] Ethelwold must be allowed a sense of humor when the preceding statement is read in the light of the acrimony that followed the reformation of the Old Minster. The assembled nobles, abbots, abbesses, bishops, and representatives from Fleury and Ghent expressed their confirmation of the document drawn up by Ethelwold (with an insertion by Dunstan), the <u>Monastic Agreement of the Monks and Nuns of the English Nation</u>.[16]

The <u>Monastic Agreement</u> is an amalgamation of foreign practices based on the Rule of St. Benedict and the interpolations of Benedict of Aniane, interpreted and expanded to meet the special needs of English monasticism. Ethelwold's treatise must not be viewed as a mere copy of foreign models, as Frederick Tupper noted: "I have not felt, however, in comparing the Continental documents with the English that the first were direct progenitors of the second: the connection is a more distant one."[17] Ethelwold's genius transcended mere copying. One of his original contributions is the inclusion in the <u>Monastic Agreement</u> of the rubrics of the <u>Visitation to the Sepulchre,</u> which perhaps had been performed in conventual churches since his days at Abingdon.

The <u>Monastic Agreement</u> contains a lengthy preface which explains Edgar's reasons for convoking the synod and several admonishments on the proper conduct of the monastic life. Then follow several chapters of descriptions of liturgies and monastic duties. The language of the <u>Monastic Agreement</u> is, of course, Latin, but it is important to note that it contains "a sprinkling of Greek forms in Latin dress."[18]

Ethelwold and his collaborators realized that monastic life in England differed from communal life in more temperate European countries; they made provisions accordingly for strictly English needs. For instance, the monks were allowed a fire in a special room in winter and could elect to work indoors if the weather demanded. English custom favored the extensive use of bells on ceremonial occasions, so special concessions were made to that predilection. The monks were enjoined to celebrate the Mass daily, possibly in accordance with the advice of the Venerable Bede. The most striking innovation of the English reformers, however, was instituting the royal family as patrons of the religious establishment, a move which had no counterpart in European monasticism. The phenomenon of monastic cathedrals, moreover, is purely English. These examples should suffice to convince skeptics that Ethelwold produced a document with a curiously national flavor, that he felt free to experiment with traditional practices, and that he faced unique problems and produced novel solutions. "In the past of England the monastic body had had a share in the national life without parallel elsewhere, and the characteristics of the past revived in the century before the Conquest during which the Church and State in England intermingled their functions in a manner wholly unique."[19]

The similarity of the <u>Monastic Agreement</u> to the Rule of St. Benedict can be suggested by setting down the chapter headings:

1. Of the Manner in Which the Customs of the Regular Life Ought to Be Observed by Monks Day and Night throughout the Year.
2. Of the Order of the Hymns in Winter; and of the Manner in Which Certain Other Monastic Duties Shall Be Fulfilled.

Plate I. Title Page of the **Monastic Agreement**
From the Cotton MS. Tiberius A3 fol. 2b

3. Of the Manner in Which the Vigil of Christmas Shall Fittingly Be Kept; and of the Period from That Solemnity until Septuagesima.
4. Of the Order of the Regular Life from Septuagesima to the End of Lent.
5. Of the Manner in Which the Day and Night Office Shall Be Carried out on the Feast of Easter.
6. Of the Manner in Which Saturday, the Octave of Easter, and the Whole Summer Time Shall Be Kept.
7. Of the Manner in Which the Brother Who Is Called _Circa_ Shall Fulfill His Office.
8. Of the Manner in Which the Day and Night Office Shall be Carried out in Whit Week.
9. Of the Manner in Which the Quarter Tense Days Shall Be Kept.
10. Of the Order in Which the Daily Maundy Shall Be Offered to the Poor by the Brethren; and in What Manner the Abbot Shall Entertain Strangers.
11. Of the Order in Which the Brethren Shall Carry out the _Munditiae_ on Saturday; and of Certain Duties Which They Shall Perform for the Good of Their Souls.
12. Of the Care of a Sick Brother; and of the Manner in Which the Dead Shall Be Committed to the Earth.
Here the Chapters End. [20]

For the sake of subsequent discussion, some matters must be extrapolated from the _Monastic Agreement._ First, it is noted in Ch. I, 17 that after the brethren complete their private devotions, a bell is rung to summon the boys. [21] These children are members of the monastic school, some of them given in infancy to be monks, other in attendance merely to be educated. St. Benedict's Rule and the _Monastic Agreement_ make many provisions for these boys, who figure prominently in considering the identity of the audience of the Easter play. In Ch. I, 19 these boys are referred to as the _schola_ and their teacher as _magister._ [22] Ch. I, 20[23] confirms that the choir sat on opposite sides of the presbytery and sang antiphonally, facts that corroborate some of the stage directions of the play.

After Tierce, bells were rung to call the faithful together for the Mass (Ch. I, 23), [24] and both Symons[25] and Knowles[26] assume that _fidelem aduocantes plebem missam incohent_ means that a lay congregation celebrated Mass with the monks. That belief is unwarranted because the _Monastic Agreement_ contains clear directions for services celebrated by monks and the laity. For example, Ch. III, 33 discusses the manner of processing from the monastery to a parish church on the feast of the Purification of Mary. [27] The brethren are advised to walk silently and dress in albs if the weather permits. After certain rites in the parish church, the monks are to walk back to the abbey church with lighted tapers and sing additional responses for the sacrifice of the Mass. Thus the _Monastic Agreement_ suggests that when the commons' presence with the monks was desirable, they came together in parish churches, not in convents. Similar festal processions to extra-conventual churches are countenanced in Ch. IV, 34.[28] The greatest procession of the Holy Year transpired on Palm Sunday (Ch. IV, 36),[29] with a small procession inside the cloister and a grander one to a neighborhood church.

On Maundy Thursday a symbolic representation is allowed for those monks whose spirituality would be strengthened thereby. As Ethelwold says, "Therefore it seemed good to us to insert these things so that if there be any to whose devotion they are pleasing, they may find therein the means of instructing those who are ignorant of this matter...."[30] After the singing of the night office when all the lights have been extinguished, two boys should stand on the right of the choir and sing clearly Kyrie eleison; two boys on the left answer with Christe eleison; and to the west of the choir (that is, from the direction of the main doors) stand two boys who sing Lord, have mercy on us, to which the choir answers, Christ the Lord is made obedient even unto death. Then the whole ceremony, enacted in remembrance of Christ's agony in the garden before His arrest, is repeated a second and a third time, followed by prayers and silent meditation, a ritual which is repeated on three successive nights. The importance of this cultic rite rests in the fact that Ethelwold had the imagination and the freedom to add extra-liturgical practices to the regimen as a means of strengthening the spiritual resolution of his flock. He introduced the liturgical music-drama for the same purpose and with the same ingenuity.

Ethelwold's acquaintance with the Greek language is germane to the following chapters. According to the Monastic Agreement, at the hour of None on Good Friday, two deacons hold aloft the Cross while certain liturgical formulae are repeated in Latin and Greek.[31] English monks, then, were expected to be familiar with Greek responses probably learned by rote; in this respect Ethelwold's gift of the Book of Greek Letters to Peterborough is significant.

Ch. IV, 46[32] describes the Easter sepulchre. The nature and location of the simulated tomb are suggested by the text: "...sit autem in una parte altaris, qua vacuum fuerit...." E.K. Chambers, claiming that the Latin is atrocious, says that the tomb was on the altar, not in the hollow of it.[33] Thomas Symons translates the clause in this way: "...on that part of the altar where there is a space for it...,"[34] thus appearing to agree with Chambers. Two responses to their positions are necessary. First of all, the Latin is quite clear and grammatical; the passage says, "Let there be, however, in one part of the altar where there is an empty space ..." Both writers err, perhaps, in viewing the altar merely as a table; the context suggests that Ethelwold referred to the entire altar area, which often involved the table itself set on a raised platform. Martin Biddle, in fact, discovered archaeological evidence that the altar in the renovated Old Minster was situated on a dais elevated above the level of the presbytery floor;[35] possibly a similar arrangement existed when the Easter music-drama first was presented.

The actual description of the Visitation to the Sepulchre appears in Ch. V, 51.[36] Since the dramatic event itself is the subject of a later chapter, some generalizations about the Monastic Agreement are pertinent now.

First, the tone of the document, as well as Benedictine tradition, suggests that its compiler felt considerable freedom to experiment with liturgical and extra-liturgical forms of worship. The presence of the Easter play in the Monastic Agreement is an ingenious but not a particularly unprecedented addition to the liturgy, given the previous prevalence of troping.

Second, the fact that the Monastic Agreement represents a strictly English interpretation (albeit with European influences) of the Rule of St. Benedict and related traditions suggests that the drama was of English provenance. Why else does a drama not appear in an earlier continental manuscript?

Third, the Monastic Agreement doubtless includes monastic ceremonies already in effect in some English monasteries at the time of the composition of the document. The Winchester Easter play, consequently, may have been introduced at any date after 946, the year in which Ethelwold became Abbot of Abingdon.

Fourth, regardless of the date of the introduction of the play in the English houses, the Monastic Agreement, by virtue of being sanctioned by both Church and State, insured that the play would be produced throughout England every Easter until 980 (the year the Vikings recommenced their raids) and thereafter whenever possible until the Norman Archbishop of Canterbury, Lanfranc (1070-89), brought English monasteries in line with contemporary Gallic customs. Before religious trends initiated in the tenth-century were disrupted by foreign invasion, both by the Vikings and by the Normans, Benedictinism fostered a period of significant activity, especially in cultural matters.

Notes

[1] L. M. Smith, The Early History of the Monastery of Cluny (London, 1920), p. 3, n. 1.

[2] David Knowles, The Monastic Order in England, 2nd ed. (Cambridge, 1962), p. 7. According to a sixteenth-century document, the average age of a monk at profession was 16.5 years; the average duration of the monastic life was 33.5 years; and the average age at death was 50.2. See Robert Causton, "Nomina Monachorum vivorum et mortuorum Ecclesie Xpi. Cant. a tempore 1207 ad annum 1533," Ninth Report of the Historical Manuscripts Commission of Great Britain (London, 1883), I, 127.

[3] Knowles, p. 15.

[4] Knowles, p. 23.

[5] Joan Evans, Monastic Life at Cluny, 910-1157 (New York, 1968), passim.

Also see Rose Graham, "The Relation of Cluny to Some Other Movements of Monastic Reform," Journal of Theological Studies, XV (1914), 179-195.

[6] Knowles, pp. 20-30.

[7] Hunter Blair, ed. and trans., The Rule of St. Benedict (Fort Augustus, Scotland, 1948), p. 11. All subsequent citations of the Rule refer to this edition.

[8] Cuthbert Butler, Benedictine Monachism: Studies in the Benedictine Life and Rule (Cambridge, 1924), pp. 33-34.

[9] For these versions, see H. Logeman, The Rule of St. Benet. Early English Text Society, O.S. 99 (London, 1888), and Ernst A. Koch, Three Middle English Versions of the Rule of St. Benet. Early English Text Society, O.S. 120 (London, 1902).

[10] Leechdoms, Wortcunning, and Starcraft in Early England, ed. Oswald Cockayne. Rerum Britannicarum Medii Aevi Scriptores, No. 35 (London, 1886), I, 441-442; Mary Bateson, "Rules for Monks and Canons after the Revival under King Edgar," English Historical Review, IX (1894), 692.

[11] "AEthelwold's Translation of the Regula Sancti Benedicti and Its Latin Exemplar," Anglo-Saxon England 3. Ed. Peter Clemoes (Cambridge, 1974), 125-152.

[12] Reprinted in Arnold Schörer, Die Angelsächischen Prosabearbeitungen der Benedictinerregel (Kassel, 1888).

[13] Liber Eliensis, ed. E.O. Blake. Publications of the Royal Historical Society, Camden 3rd ser., XCII (London, 1962), 111.

[14] Knowles, p. 42.

[15] Regularis Concordia, ed. Thomas Symons. Nelson's Medieval Classics (London, 1953), p. 2. Subsequent citations of the Monastic Agreement refer to this edition.

[16] Only two MSS of the Monastic Agreement are extant: British Museum Cotton MS. Faustina B 3 (late 10th century) and BM Cotton MS. Tiberius A 3.

[17] Frederick Tupper, "History and Texts of the Benedictine Reform of the Tenth Century," Modern Language Notes, VIII (1893), 354.

[18] Knowles, p. 43.

[19] Knowles, p. 46; H.R. Loyn, "Church and State in England in the Tenth and Eleventh Centuries," Tenth-Century Studies, ed. David Parsons (London, 1975), pp. 94-102.

[20] Regularis Concordia, p. 10.

[21] Regularis Concordia, p. 13.

[22] Regularis Concordia, p. 14.

[23] Regularis Concordia, p. 16.

[24] Regularis Concordia, p. 19.

[25] Regularis Concordia, p. 19, n. 5.

[26] Knowles, p. 44.

[27] Regularis Concordia, pp. 30-31.

[28] Regualris Concordia, p. 32.

[29] Regularis Concordia, p. 36.

[30] Regularis Concordia, p. 37.

[31] Regularis Concordia, p. 42.

[32]Regularis Concordia, p. 44.

[33]E.K. Chambers, The Mediaeval Stage (Oxford, 1903), II, 17, n. 1.

[34]Regularis Concordia, p. 44.

[35]"The Excavation of the Old Minster," The Old Minster: Excavations near Winchester Cathedral, 1961-1969 (Winchester, 1970), p. 93.

[36]Regularis Concordia, pp. 49-50.

CHAPTER IV

THE FRUITS OF THE MONASTIC REVIVAL

Ethelwold and his associates effected a religious revival so remarkable with respect to art and architecture, learning and literature, liturgy, music, and drama that historians have dwelt upon these achievements while passing over the spiritual motives which guided the actions of the reformers. Yet, as Wickham reminds us, we need to know "the religious and artistic considerations which moved men of the Middle Ages to express themselves in drama."[1] Admittedly, it is never easy to plumb a man's spirit to ascertain how devotion, asceticism, and religious emotion drive the man of action to do good deeds or the man of intellect to produce illuminating concepts. The task is nearly impossible even when the subject leaves diaries, letters, and autobiographical materials; without such literary remains, educated speculation alone remains. Subsequent generations have made saints of Ethelwold, Dunstan, and Oswald, but aside from the grossly inaccurate, biased lives of the three bishops, there exists but little evidence, aside from external manifestations of their zeal, to reveal their motives, personalities, or daily lives. Ethelwold made no novel contribution, so far as is known, to the life of the spirit: he produced no devotional literature, wrote no great hymn of the church, conceived no sweeping theological doctrine. In his life, though, he showed his followers the fruits of the Christian spirit. Many of his reforms did not originate with him, and his Agreement contains but little which is unique; he simply drew upon existing traditions and his own imagination in response to the need of his flock for an orderly system of service to God. That he decided to show his monks the significance of the Resurrection rather than to tell them about it is a spontaneously creative act by a man of genius. The making of drama was Ethelwold's spiritual gift to Western civilization, a feat worthy of standing beside the fairest anthem, the most profound teaching, the most awesome edifice. As prolegomena to a discussion in detail of this legacy, Ethelwold's contributions to art and culture must be introduced.

Pictorial and Decorative Arts

"Winchester illumination is the first really English thing in English art."[2] The monks who created the Winchester style of manuscript illumination solved the most baffling problem in pre-Conquest art, says T. D. Kendrick, that of "combining the glittering abstract patterns of insular 'barbaric' illumination with the more substantial dignities and gentler graces of the classical tradition in painting."[3] If Winchester illumination is the best thing in Saxon art, as Kendrick claims, it is necessary to characterize that style. First, manuscripts painted in this manner contain abstract decorative elements of Celtic derivation and figure drawing in the classical (both Byzantine and Roman) manner; the balance between the two influences accounts for the main effects of the style. Second, the illustrators depicted human figures and scenes and tried to show emotion and movement, especially in the agitated flutter of draperies. [4] Third, figures, especially royalty, were portrayed more humanly than were their counterparts on the continent. Fourth, the Winchester illuminators favored exceedingly rich colors and used gold liberally in their paintings. Since many studies of these manuscripts have been published, notably those of Kendrick[5] and Rice, [6] it is superfluous to enumerate and describe the work of the Winchester scriptoria. It is necessary, on the other hand, to discuss briefly three drawings that may bear upon the production of the Easter drama.

A long Latin poem inscribed in gold capital letters introduces the Bene-dictional of St. Ethelwold: "A bishop, the great Ethelwold, whom the Lord had made patron of Winchester, ordered a certain monk subject to him to write the present book. . . . He commanded also to be made in this book many frames well adorned and filled with various figures decorated with numerous beautiful colours and with gold. . . . Let all who look upon this book pray always that after the term of the flesh I may abide in heaven--Godeman the scribe, as a suppliant, earnestly asks this. "[7] This handsome book bears on the study of liturgical music-drama because it contains a picture of the Angel and the Marys at the tomb of Jesus on Easter morning.

While there is danger in assuming that the conventions of one art form may be faithfully represented in another, W. L. Hildburgh[8] and M. D. Anderson[9] have demonstrated a relationship between medieval drama and the plastic arts, specifically alabaster carvings and sculpture. Both Hildburgh and Anderson believe that craftsmen in stone copied scenes from dramatic presentations, and they imply that pictorializations of the earliest religious plays were made and are now lost. Fletcher Collins, Jr. uses medieval sculpture to reconstruct scenes from liturgical dramas. [10] The work of these writers has been instructive, but such comparisons should be employed cautioulsy. This conservative approach dictates restraint in positing a definite relationship between contemporary illuminations and dramatic performances at Winchester.

The nature of the Easter sepulchre as described in the Monastic Agreement has been introduced previously: a simulated tomb hung with a curtain and placed in the altar area where there was room. Emile Mâle[11] states that the ancient formula for depicting the Resurrection scene provides for a tomb of two stories, similar to classical funerary monuments. The Angel sits or stands before the entrance to the tomb. The illustration from the Benedictional of St. Ethelwold, with its sepulchre based on a Byzantine prototype, [12] may suggest how the scene was envisioned in tenth-century minsters. While it is impossible to maintain that the illumination reflected the actual presentation of the play, it is helpful to compare the rubrics of the drama with the visualization of the same scene by an artist who doubtless was a member of the audience. Godeman the scribe, an inmate of the Old Minster when the benedictional was fabricated, later became Abbot of Thorney. [13]

Plate II. The Marys at the Tomb from the
Benedictional of St. Ethelwold

A similar service book, owned by Archbishop Robert of Rouen[14] was produced in the scriptorium of the New Minster between 980 and 990. The manuscript remained in England until 1020, when it was removed to France.[15] A Resurrection scene is depicted in this document as well. The Angel and Marys are remarkably similar to their counterparts in Ethelwold's benedictional, as is the border decoration. The main difference lies in the treatment of the sepulchre and the guards. The tomb in Robert's book is much plainer than that of the earlier illustration. Ethelwold's guards, standing to the left of the sepulchre, are quite alert, while the sentries sleep peacefully at the bottom of the drawing in Robert's pontifical. The similarities between the two portrayals are substantive, the dissimilarities marginal, just as two productions of the same drama might be.

A Resurrection scene also appears in the missal of Robert of Jumièges, which was illuminated in some monastery of the Winchester connection. The Angel and the Marys seem to be related to the corresponding figures in the other two books, but the border and the sepulchre are impressively dissimilar. The Marys, furthermore, stand at the left of the picture, a Syro-Palestinian convention that is not duplicated in the other drawings. Finally, no guards at all are drawn.

The artists of the three pictures may have drawn from related sources, possibly the production of the Visitation to the Sepulchre in different English monasteries. It may be significant, moreover, that the elements prescribed in the rubrics of the drama (the Angel and the Marys) were represented similarly in the paintings while those unspecified in the Monastic Agreement were depicted ad libitum. Such a mixture of freedom and restraint is not unknown in medieval art.

The Winchester style of illumination, then, was a strictly English manifestation of the artistic spirit perfected under the patronage of Ethelwold. Certainly the innovators drew from existing sources, as artists always do, but their unique manipulation of their means of mimesis make their artworks original creations. This point will be reiterated when the subject under consideration is drama, not drawing.

Sculpture

"The relationship between the reformed rule of English monasticism in the tenth century and sculpture is difficult to define largely because of certain factors inherent in the nature of the material and its production."[16] There is no reason to believe that the monks of Winchester were particularly interested in sculpting, yet the tenth-century revival affected that art in a significant manner:

Plate III. The Marys at the Tomb from the
Benedictional of Archbishop Robert

Plate IV. The Marys at the Tomb from the
Missal of Robert of Jumièges

As in earlier days, the current of influence was at this time not entirely directed from east to west. The English monastic reformers under Dunstan were independent of those at Cluny and may have influenced the continent even if later the Cluniac ideas came to exercise an important effect on Britain. And in the sphere of manuscript illumination there was a good deal of English influence in France.... It may even be that the sudden growth in the importance of sculpture on the continent at this time came about to some extent as the result of English inspiration, for this country was in advance of the continent at least with regard to the quality of the work that was being produced.[17]

Kendrick and Rice present enough examples to convince one that in the tenth century "England was in the forefront as a centre of religious sculpture..,"[18] so it is unnecessary to discuss individual works. A few generalizations about Anglo-Saxon sculpture and its sources are, however, in order.

Scandinavian influences predominated in Northern English art until the Conquest; consequently, the most indigenous sculpture comes from the south of England. The center of sculpting activity moved southward, so that in the tenth century, Wessex produced the finest stonework in England. Even in Alfred's day, a court school produced imposing works, and in the age of Edgar sculpture reached its zenith, with Ethelwold's influence doubtless a factor. Knowledge of Saxon sculpture is limited because stone, wood, stucco, and metal have been lost through deterioration or willful destruction.[19] It may be surprising to some to learn that Saxon sculpture frequently was painted. As Cramp points out, Saxon sculpture was largely educational: " ... [T]he wall paintings and stone carvings in churches, and the sculpture of crosses were for the enlightenment of the unlettered... this was the way in which the ordinary man and woman in the countryside became aware, as a supplement to sermons he may not have swiftly grasped, of the spread of new theological ideas.'[20] In this, sculpture was akin to drama.

The drama's debt to Byzantine influences is germane to the next chapter, a relationship that is also apparent in Anglo-Saxon sculpture. According to Rice, "It was Byzantine art...that was behind the tenth-century revival in Britain...."[21] The winged angel in the church at Deerhurst, a tenth-century monastery, is noticeably affected by a Byzantine model, as well as by Celtic influences, as are the carved flying angels in the churches of Bradford-on-Avon and Winterbourne Steepleton. These angels are quite similar to those depicted in the Benedictional of St. Ethelwold. The Romsey Rood was also inspired by Byzantine crucifixes; the monastic reformers instituted a nunnery at Romsey. In addition there are scores of carved figures that bear some relation to the art of Byzantium, as do ivory carvings and works in metal.

English craftsmen were renowned for their ivory work and gold and silver artifacts. Unfortunately many of the precious ecclesiastical vessels of the tenth century were melted down to supply tribute to the Conqueror from Normandy. "From documentary sources it is clear that there were many grand treasures in the churches of England in the tenth century but none of these survive [sic] in this country. "[22] A crozier mount in Cologne, a portable altar in Cluny, and three bronze censer-covers in England are all the extant religious artifacts of the Monastic Revival; secular relics are not much more abundant. Yet it is known that many fine pieces existed and that Dunstan himself was the patron saint of jewellers and silversmiths; he also produced textile designs to be embroidered by a wealthy woman named Ethelbyra. Indeed, English artisans were reputed to be cunning workers in textiles, the most impressive remains of which are the St. Cuthbert fabrics, executed between 909 and 916. These masterpieces of weaving and embroidery also reflect Byzantine influence, which, says Rice, was far more crucial to the development of English art than was that of the Northmen. [23]

"The picture of the age as presented by the arts is thus one of gradual penetration of new ideas, sponsored first by the court and then by the church, till eventually a definite idiom in the new style was achieved about the year 950. This idiom was then developed and disseminated as something fresh and vital .... "[24] This conclusion is particularly applicable to the art produced in the cloisters of the Winchester connection, which developed a distinctly Romanesque character a century before that style began to flourish in Burgundy and France. Indeed, Ethelwold created an atmosphere in Winchester that was conducive to artistic expression.

The Architecture of the Monastic Revival

The monastic reformers did not neglect the erection of churches. Despite the fact that houses of worship were built usually of timber and that old churches were demolished to make room for new structures, nearly two hundred Saxon or partially-Saxon places of worship remain. While secular churches are not direct concerns of this study, their features provide important keys to architectural conventions in conventual churches. [25] The architecture of Ethelwold's cathedral in Winchester--the scene of the production of the Easter music-drama -- is of paramount importance.

In 1957 R. N. Quirk published a remarkably prescient article in which he augmented the existing documentary references to the Old Minster with far-ranging hypotheses of his own in an attempt to describe the church as it existed in Ethelwold's day. [26] His timetable for the building of the cathedral helps to clarify the confusing stages of the development of Ethelwold's see:

A.D.	971	Translation of St. Swithun's bones from his tomb outside.
	980	Dedication of the first part of the work of reconstruction and restoration of the Old Minster -- apparently the nave and the west end.
	984	Death of Ethelwold.
	983-4	Second dedication, under Bishop Alphege [Elfheah], of the completed works of restoration -- namely an eastern porticus, a crypt and a tower.
	996	Translation of Ethelwold's bones from the crypt into the church.
	1005	Alphege becomes Archbishop of Canterbury. [27]

Quirk's description of the reconstruction of the Old Minster is based on the accounts of Lantfred, Wulfstan, and AElfric, all contemporaries of Ethelwold, so their comments must be somewhat authoritative. Certain miracles at the grave of St. Swithun persuaded Ethelwold that new provisions ought to be made for the saint's relics. On 15 July 971 Ethelwold presided over a procession of choir-boys whose songs were somewhat marred by an approaching storm. The officiating monks erected a screen around the grave of Swithun, then proceeded once again into the church. Upon their return, the grave covering was removed and the coffin exhumed and moved to a more fitting place. Between the tomb and the church (on the east) was a stone cross, and at the west of the grave was a tower dedicated to St. Martin. On 22 October 974 a second translation of the saint's remains to a more suitable receptacle was made. The sanctified remnants were housed in a spendid reliquary of silver, gems, and three hundred pounds of gold, which was placed in a locked and guarded enclosure. Pilgrims presumably strained their necks to view the reliquary, which was somehow raised above their heads. Quirk guesses that only part of Swithun's relics were housed in this shrine. The remainder of his bones was placed in a portable reliquary which was stored under the high altar by either 980 or 993-94.

The exact nature of the construction superintended by Ethelwold is not clarified by reading the contradictory sources. Quirk suggests that Ethelwold built some form of west-works, which might have had a variety of functions: a gallery for singers; the site of an important altar; the location of royal pews; an area from which the inmates of the Nunnaminster might view the services; an ecclesiastical court; west-choirs for antiphonal singing; a segregated chapel for the laity.

Quirk's article is admirable because his conclusions, based solely on documentary evidence, have largely been corroborated by excavations at the site of the Old Minster, which is the only Saxon cathedral to be unearthed and studied systematically. The story of these diggings reads like detective fiction but demonstrates that ancient authorities were not as inaccurate as sometimes represented. [28]

In 1960 plans for the erection of a new hotel on the site of the Cathedral parking lot were announced. Under the leadership of Quirk, arrangements were made to investigate the archaeological remains in that area prior to the modern construction; the project was to be directed by Martin Biddle and subsidized by the City Council, the Ministry of Works, the Society of Antiquaries, and an anonymous benefactor.

The preliminary diggings in 1961 disclosed that Roman as well as medieval levels were in evidence. East of a cemetery beneath the parking lot, an oval-shaped building, later identified as a chapel with eastern and western apses (a Byzantine idea), was found. No similar buildings had been unearthed in England or abroad. [29]

In 1962 the Winchester Excavations Committee was formed to superintend the greatly enlarged plan for studying the site. The archaeologists determined to locate the Old and New Minsters by digging trenches adjacent to the present nave. In one of these trenches were the tenth-century remains of decorated, glazed tiles which are "quite unlike any known medieval tiles in glaze, fabric, and decoration."[30] Three hundred years separated those tiles and similar ones anywhere in Europe. A great stone coffin was discovered in the floor of the first of two levels, indicating an ecclesiastical burial place. It was deduced that the site of the Old Minster had been found.

The excavations of 1963 verified Roman as well as Saxon ruins on the site. Numerous trenches tentatively suggested that parts of both minsters had been located, but corroboration of this thesis was postponed until the following summer. In 1964 Biddle and his associates discovered that the Old Minster partly underlies the nave of the present cathedral. The Old Minster was demolished in 1093, beginning on the day after the consecration of the new Norman church; therefore demolition and construction were being carried on simultaneoulsy. The archaeological team began to suspect that William of Malmesbury had not exaggerated the closeness of the two minsters. A grown man barely could walk between their walls. It was evident, furthermore, that the Old Minster was a building of great size and complexity.

That Ethelwold's church was remodeled in two stages was determined in 1965, a discovery that confirmed the documentary sources. Ethelwold's new church was dedicated in 980, and the eastern construction was consecrated in 993-94. Diggings in 1965 also confirmed the proximity of the two monasteries and that the New Minster was built upon the cemetery of the Old Minster.

In 1966 the shape of the Old Minster was determined finally, but "the form of the building is so strange and unexpected that it seems to raise more questions than it has answered."[31] The church was 159 feet long, with an aisleless nave, 24 feet wide internally, which was entered from the elevated forecourt by steps. The nave extended ten feet west of the facade, which was 102 feet wide with flanking north and south porticūs. "This colossal structure must

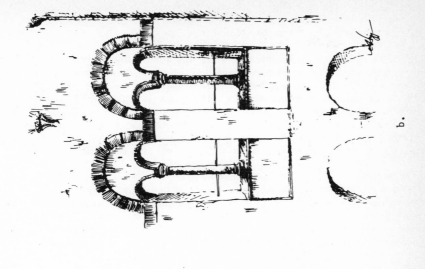

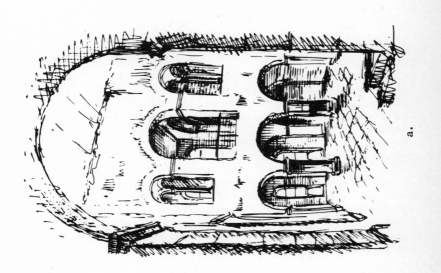

Fig. 2. West-works: facing west (a) and facing north (b)

have been one of the architectural wonders of the Anglo-Saxon kingdom and have dominated the city as does the Norman Cathedral today."[32] The position of the high altar was emphasized by its standing directly in the center of the axis of the easternmost north-south porticus. A confessio, built on the foundation of an earlier chapel, sat beneath the high altar, which was reached by a flight of steps. The east end of the church terminated in an apse with an external crypt.

The New Minster church was architecturally quite different from the Old Minster. Consecrated in 903, it was built along continental lines with an aisled nave, 119 feet long and 68 feet wide with "shallow eastern transepts, projecting ten feet beyond the aisles."[33] On a block in the south wall of the New Minster, the excavators found a stone with a ninth-century painting in the Carolingian manner, the only significant extant example of Saxon wall painting. This picture is similar in some respects to the painting in the Benedictional of St. Ethelwold, so a relationship between illumination and wall painting may some day be established.

By the end of the tenth century, the facade of the Old Minster, looking down on the forecourt with its ranks of tombs and central monument, and, to the north, the jutting front of the New Minster, with nearby its six-storied tower, must have composed one of the grandest architectural settings in Europe. With the royal palace flanking the western side of the court, it is clear that we stand here at the architectural heart of the Saxon kingdom. [34]

The excavations in 1967 showed that some misinterpretations of the evidence had been made, but the summer's work resulted in establishing an outline of the development of the Old Minster and St. Swithun's shrine from the seventh to the tenth century. In 1968 Biddle's hypothetical sequence of the stages of the building seemed justified, but actual confirmation was postponed until the next summer.

The work of 1969 resolved the various conflicting theories and showed that some of Biddle's conjectures of 1967 had been erroneous. By 1970 three-fourths of the Old Minster had been unearthed; the remainder lay beneath the present cathedral. The assumption that the south side of the Old Minster mirrored the north is not unlikely, so it is possible to reconstruct the ground plan of the Old Minster.

The church built upon the site in 648 by Cenwalch was cruciform. An isolated rectangular building west of the west front of the church has been identified as St. Martin's tower, since its location agrees with the documentary evidence. Lying on the axis of the church and St. Martin's tower is the site of St. Swithun's grave of 971. The laterally-apsed buildings that connect the tower with the cruciform church were built at some time after 971. The apses are so massive that it seems that they enclosed a shrine dedicated to Winchester's most popular saint, Swithun. The actual gravesite was enclosed by a three-

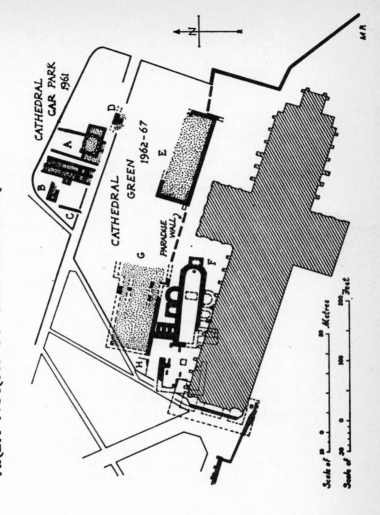

Fig. 3. Excavations near Winchester Cathedral

sided chamber which possibly contained a reliquary after the second translation of Swithun's relics in 974.

A rectangular west-works was added prior to 984. The exact function of this new structure is not known, but it is supposed that the addition was necessary because the huge shrine-church could not be roofed satisfactorily or properly supported. On the other hand, the new west-works might have met some special liturgical requirements and served some special needs as part of the most important church in the kingdom, thus uniting ecclesiastical and governmental functions.

The east end of the church was dedicated in 993-94. The eastern additions included "the eastern crypt and apse, the north and south apses at the east end, and the formation of a new crypt in the original east end, below the new, and now raised, high altar."[35] The date of the lateral wings nearest the west front has not been established with certainty.

Many problems defy solution, and final judgments must await expert interpretaions of the evidence, but at this point, it is justifiable to say that Ethelwold's architectural vision was perfectly congruent with his achievements in the other arts. Indeed, the Old and New Minsters were fitting homes for the music-drama.

Learning and Literature

These artistic accomplishments were simply manifestations of Ethelwold's main concern, which was educational as well as devotional. His goal was to train a clergy, both secular and regular, competent to instruct the people and deliver the country from the intellectual and religious turmoil which had prevailed throughout the dark period of the Danish wars. Education, especially of monks, was the key to saving England from the dark ages.

Every Benedictine monastery had a school, and the model for Ethelwold's schools came from ninth-century France. Two kinds of monastic schools flourished at Fleury after 855; the claustral school for oblates and the canonical school for secular clerks and laymen of noble birth.[36] That Ethelwold took delight in teaching in his schools is a matter of record.[37]

The curriculum of the Winchester schools has not survived, but a document known as St. Dunstan's Classbook from Glastonbury[38] lists the subjects taught in monastic scholae. The first part of the manuscript is a work by Eutychus on the conjugation of Latin verbs; it is followed by a homily on the invention of the cross. The longest section contains a treatise on numbers and alphabets, an essay on reckoning the date of Easter, a description of the course of the moon, a lunar table, a paschal chart, a treatise on the calculus, a dis-

WINCHESTER, THE OLD MINSTER
INTERPRETATION 1967

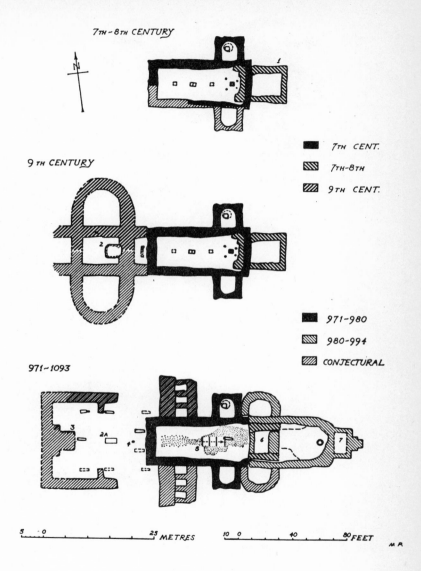

7TH – 8TH CENTURY

9 TH CENTURY

■ 7TH CENT.

▨ 7TH-8TH

▨ 9TH CENT.

971–1093

■ 971–980

▨ 980–994

▨ CONJECTURAL

5   0   25 METRES   10 0   40   80 FEET

M R

Fig. 4. Sequential Development of the Old Minster

Plate V. Dunstan before Christ from St. Dunstan's
Classbook from Glastonbury

The inscription says, "I pray you, gentle Christ, to watch over me,
Dunstan, that you not allow the hurricanes of hell to swallow me."

cussion of weights and measures, the multiplication tables, and liturgical lessons in Latin and Greek based on works by Bede, Isidore, Nemnivus, and Victorius of Aquitaine. The fourth section contains the first book of Ovid's Art of Love. The first, second, and fourth parts were copied by the same hand; sections three and four were certainly with Dunstan at Glastonbury or Canterbury. Assuming that similar matters occupied the students at Winchester, one may conclude that the boys received an excellent education for their time, especially when it is remembered that the normal tutorials were augmented by studies of the Bible, the Rule, and the Church Fathers.

Neither Dunstan nor Oswald left any writings. To Ethelwold can be attributed the English translation of the Rule, the composition of the Monastic Agreement, and the vernacular account of the founding of the monasteries.[39] Yet, the Monastic Revival was largely literary and resulted in the composition of numerous Latin works and, more importantly, in establishing English as a literary language:

> It was only then [during the Monastic Revival] that English monastic life was finally restored and that English culture and scholarship regained something of the brilliance which had once emanated from the Northumbrian monasteries, and only then that the conditions were created for the composition of the great Anglo-Saxon prose works at the end of the tenth century. It seems a logical step to presume further that this reform movement was also a driving force in the evolution and diffusion of a literary language.[40]

Helmut Gneuss believes that Ethelwold's patronage of learning at the Old Minster provided the regulation and cultivation necessary to the ripening and dissemination of Standard Old English as a literary tongue. Indeed, he calls Ethelwold and his scholarly circle at Winchester "England's first English philologists."[41] The literary fruits of the Monastic Revival appeared after the deaths of the reforming bishops, but Ethelwold proved to have been a good teacher, as did his colleagues.

AElfric the Grammarian (c. 950- c. 1020) was a student of Ethelwold at the Old Minster. Nothing is known of his life until he was sent in 987 by Elfheah to teach the monks at Cerne. Thereupon AElfric produced two sets of homilies, the first doctrinal, the second historical. Possibly after his return to Winchester, AElfric wrote a Latin grammar, a Latin-English wordbook, and the Colloquy, a list of everyday terms to be memorized by schoolboys at the monastery. Around 997 AElfric wrote a third set of homilies based on the lives of saints particularly venerated by monks. Around 998 he undertook the translation of the Old Testament for preachers. He and his co-workers wrote paraphrases of the Pentateuch and extracts from Judges, Job, Esther, and Judith. After 998 he penned two long letters describing the traditional beliefs of the church.

AElfric became Abbot of Eynsham, a new monastery, in 1005. For his community he abridged the Monastic Agreement, and in 1005/6 he wrote his Life of Ethelwold. Abbot AElfric also wrote an essay on the Old and New Testaments and a letter in favor of clerical celibacy for a friend named Sigeferth. Around 1014-16 he drafted another pastoral letter and translated it into English. The remaining years of England's greatest medieval educator, with the possible exception of Bede, were spent in meditation and reading.

Byrhtferth, mainly a writer of scientific documents, lived at Ramsey and preserved the traditions of Fleury. Wulfstan of York, a homilist, was Bishop of York and Worcester after leaving the cloister at Winchester. His Sermon of the Wolf to the English is anthologized frequently. AElfric of Bath translated the gospels into English, and another AElfric ("the Bat") published the Grammarian's Colloquy with his own emendations.

Wulfstan of Winchester wrote on musical subjects, while Lantfred of Winchester described the miracles of St. Swithun. AElfward, Abbot of Glastonbury, wrote a pastoral epistle to Sigeric of Canterbury. All these writers came under the influence of Ethelwold, as did the author(s) of the poems of the Winchester school described by Michael Lapidge.[42] Furthermore, the Anglo-Saxon Chronicle was written in this period largely by monks of Winchester, Abingdon, and Worcester. The anonymous Blicking Homilies (970-80), of Winchester provenance, provide insight into the daily lives of English people. A survey of literature, both religious and secular, produced between the age of Edgar and the Conquest led Peter Clemoes to call the corpus of those works "unique in the European vernaculars of the time."[43] In view of this accomplishment, Ethelwold succeeded magnificently in his goal of providing educated leadership for the English church. After 965 most English archibshops and bishops were monks; a majority of secular priests had been taught in monasteries; so the monks controlled the church and influenced temporal government. Education was solely a monastic concern, and Ethelwold's contribution was incalculable.

Liturgy, Music, and Drama

The liturgical observances of the early Christian church must habe been fairly unified, but in the fourth century a numer of occurrences precipitated ritualistic diversity: (1) the recognition of Christianity as the official religion of the Roman Empire ushered in a period of liturgical experimentation; (2) in liturgical formulae, Greek was replaced by vernacular languages -- Latin, Syriac, and Coptic; (3) the movement toward division of the Empire into eastern and western branches presaged a similar schism of the church; (4) widespread doctrinal heresies produced conflicting interpretations of the Christian message. When the Ostrogoths and Visigoths were coalesced into the Frankish kindgom, their view of the faith differed from that of orthodox Rome; nevertheless the Germanic peoples eventually controlled the remnant of the Western Roman Empire.[44]

As a result of these factors, two streams (with offshoots) of liturgical practice flowed from the same source: the Roman-African and the Gallican. The Roman eventually was ascendant, but not before it was modified by Gallican influences. At an early date music had become an integral part of Christian worship, so it is nearly impossible to speak of liturgy without referring to music as well. From the Byzantine Church, the Gallican liturgists borrowed antiphonal psalm-singing; the use of hymns also migrated from east to west. Antiphony, of course, is clearly related to liturgical music-drama, but, perhaps unexpectedly, religious drama owes a debt to hymn-singing too. The lyrics of antiphons usually were derived from the Psalms, but the desire to incorporate hymns into the liturgy necessitates the composition of new poetic texts. Once the freedom to embellish a rite is granted, a precedent that may lead to troping and even liturgical music-drama is established. The Gallican liturgy is, moreover, more opulent and dramatic than the Roman rite, but, for a number of reasons, the Roman form supplanted the Gallican.

The Frankish kingdom was the scene of contention for supremacy between the Roman and Gallican observances, but in the eighth century, Charlemagne settled the question. He applied to Rome for service-books (sacramentaries) to guide liturgical celebrations. When they arrived, he discovered that their coverage of the Christian year was incomplete; moreover they contained no musical notation, so the chants could not be learned. To remedy the first he appointed his chief educator, Alcuin the Englishman, to supplement the texts; as antidote to the second, Charlemagne imported Roman singers to teach the chants to Frankish choristers. Alcuin consulted local liturgical sources, which were Gallican, so his emendation ot the sacramentary was a somewhat Gallicanized Roman observance. Charlemagne also brought in Byzantine singers, whose chants and methods of performance also found their way into the accepted liturgy. Eventually the Roman rite came to be considered normative for the Church Universal, but not in the tenth century.

The English church was not untouched by this assimilative process. Indeed, English liturgies were amalgamations of many strains. From Benedictinism came a preference for Roman forms; from Celtic monasticism came ritual austerity; the Gallican persuasion found its way back to England; and there was the ubiquitous presence of Byzantine liturgists. During the Monastic Revival, though, the influence of Benedict was paramount, The monk, according to Benedict, is primarily a liturgist. "The monks of Winchester, Glastonbury, Ramsey, and the other refounded abbeys copied liturgical manuscripts, expressed their devotion in holy week and Easter with new ceremonies and processions, and re-edited their sacramentaries."[45] By the tenth century, a time in which liturgical embellishment was rampant, at least five different service-books were required for the celebration of the Mass and the Hours: the sacramentary, antiphonal, epistle book, gospel book, and troper. English monks studied and collated various liturgical manuals then in use, and their service-books are compendia of the Gelasian, Gallican, Gregorian, and Carolingian rites. [46] A surprising number of these books have survived.

The Lanalet pontifical (a book of episcopal blessings) composed for an English bishop, shows both Celtic and Carolingian influences. In addition to describing several ceremonies, the document contains a prescription of excommunication, apparently from the monastery of Lanalet, later St. German's. The bulk of the manuscript, though, suggests that if was compiled for use at Wells.

The pontifical of Egbert, Archbishop of York (732-66), was collated in the last half of the tenth century in the north of England. Another pontifical traditionally has borne the name of St. Dunstan,[47] but it was written just after Dunstan's death for Bishop Wulfsige III of Sherborne (992-1001). Historians value this book because it is indicative of liturgical practices at Canterbury in the period immediately following Dunstan's death.

The Benedictional of St. Ethelwold,[48] called "the greatest surviving artistic monument of the Anglo-Saxon monastic reform movement,"[49] contains only episcopal blessings for use at various feasts of the liturgical year. Ethelwold's benedictional and a similar one owned by Robert of Rouen were introduced previously in this study.

In addition to the foregoing pontificals intended for the use of bishops, some tenth-century service books for priests, called missals, have survived: the Leofric missal (early 10th century) was illustrated at Glastonbury; the missal of Robert of Jumièges was assembled before 1044, the year Robert became Bishop of London; the Red Book of Derby was written probably in the New Minster shortly after 1061. The last-named missals post-date the period under discussion, but they were results of the same forces that led to the composition of the Monastic Agreement.

A number of psalters and gospel books of English provenance reveal some aspects of English worship.[50] The Bosworth Psalter, designed for Benedictine use, possibly for Dunstan himself, is typical of these.[51] All the preceding documents confirm the judgment that the English liturgy of the tenth century was elaborate and highly dramatic, which was partially due to the music employed in these rites.

"No great monument of liturgical verse can be ascribed to the monastic followers of Dunstan and AEthelwold,"[52] but they partook of the richness of European church music, which was then monophonic (having a single melodic line). Since a method of musical notation had not been devised, the only way that chants could be transmitted was by trained singers' teaching the tunes to other choristers. Singing schools were founded at the Swiss Abbey of St. Gall and at Metz Cathedral, from which singing-teachers went out and spread the methods of Gregorian plainchant. Authentic Roman chant was modified by regional differences and outside influences, such as that of the Byzantine choral tradition. Both the Mass and the Canonical Hours were enriched by musical elements that soon gained the force of tradition.

The repertory of chants was considerably enlarged in the Carolingian period, so that the tenth century was regarded as the "Silver Age of Plainchant." Hoppin observes that "the later additions to the plainchant repertory reflect new artistic ideals and new compositional patterns. They are not necessarily inferior simply because they differ from more ancient chant."[53] In addition to creating new chants, liturgists embellished existing musical pieces by a process called "troping," a concept that has engendered much controversy. In all probability, tropes originated in the French Abbey of St. Martial of Limoges.[54] An equally persuasive alternative is the Swiss Abbey of St. Gall, but the origin of the trope is not central to this discussion. Tropes were used to expand every element of the Mass except the Credo, but they appeared less often in the Hours. When employed there, they usually occurred "in the Vesper responsory, the last responsory of Matins, or the responsories at the end of each Nocturn."[55] Three types of trope can be identified: those that extend the melody of an existing chant; those that add a new text to an old melody; and those that feature a completely new text and new music. "Whether they were written in poetry or prose, tropes were rarely independent literary compositions."[56] Related to the trope is the embellishment called the sequence, which eventually became a completely separate musical composition. The sequence was so popular that about 4,500 were composed during the Middle Ages.

Sequences were certainly sung in English churches of the tenth century. Troping in general was especially popular in England, as was antiphonal singing. Two Winchester tropers, both from the Old Minster, one dating from the age of Ethelwold,[57] "show that in addition to the full body of plain chant the English monasteries made use not only of the elaborate additional modulations which interpolated and prolonged the important parts of the chant of the Mass and the Office, but also of a system of <u>organa</u> or polyphony which indeed shows a greater development in England than anywhere else abroad."[58] A.E. Planchart has collected and studied the entire repertory of Winchester tropes, and he concludes:

> The evolution of the Winchester trope repertory ... shows a tightening of the liturgical structure of the Troper itself, as well as a search for authoritative versions of the pieces to be copied .... Such a search, with its implication of manuscript comparisons and of scholarship (even if not in the modern sense), is entirely in keeping with the spirit of the AEthelwoldian reform, for we must remember that it was AEthelwold who sent monks of Abingdon to Fleury and Corbie to learn about monastic observance and liturgical chant.... At the same time, we must recall that the advice of the continental monks was sought not to supplant an English practice but to strengthen and to confirm a reform that had its origin within the English church and retained its English character until the first quarter of the 11th century.[59]

About English polyphonic music, less is known. The Winchester troper CC contains a collection of written-out <u>organa</u>. As Planchart says, "Had we any doubt of the intellectual thrust of these works, the rubrics to many of the organa would dispel them with statements such as Organa dulcisona docto modulamine compta, "[60] which means "elegant sweet-sounding organa with a learned melody."

Evidently Ethelwold's monks made considerable progress in music between the date at which singers from Corbie were imported to teach chant[61] and the composition of the earlier Winchester troper. English monasteries also excelled in the plainsong of the treble voices of boys, a practice that was perfected to such an extent that present-day usage has not varied greatly from Winchester's.

Some English monastic churches used organs in their services. Dunstan performed upon the instrument, and Ethelwold built an organ with his own hands and presented it to the abbey church at Abingdon. Although medieval organs resembled modern calliopes, they produced "a pure 'organ tone' capable of great crescendos and of delicate diminuendos and also capable of producing music with rhythm and of variable tempo."[62] Wulfstan says that a great organ, probably begun in Ethelwold's time, was dedicated in the Old Minster by Elfheah, Ethelwold's successor. This mighty instrument, which was played by two monks at two keyboards, was activated by twenty-six bellows arranged in two rows. Seventy men were required to operate the instrument, which had four hundred pipes. "Like thunder the iron voice batters the ear, so that it may receive no other sound. So much does it sound and resound that every one stops his gaping ears with his hands.... The music of the pipes is heard throughout the town, and the flying fame thereof is gone out over the whole country."[63] When the monks in both minsters sang the Offices, the din was disturbing to both groups, but doubtless the services accompanied by the great organ were dominant. One deduces, therefore, that ceremonies in the cloistered communities at Winchester were characterized by beauty, opulence, scholarship, and impressive sights and sounds -- an atmosphere not unsuited to dramatic performances.

Notes

[1]Glynne Wickham, Shakespeare's Dramatic Heritage: Collected Studies in Mediaeval, Tudor and Shakespearean Drama (London, 1969), p. 9.

[2]T. D. Kendrick, Late Saxon and Viking Art (London, 1949), p. 2.

[3]Kendrick, pp. 1-2.

[4]Francis Wormald, English Drawings of the Tenth and Eleventh Centuries (London, 1952), p. 24.

[5]Late Saxon and Viking Art.

[6]D. Talbot Rice, English Art, 871-1100 (Oxford, 1952).

[7]Translated in J. J. G. Alexander, "The Benedictional of St. AEthelwold & Anglo-Saxon Illumination of the Reform Period," Tenth-Century Studies, ed. David Parsons (London. 1975), p. 169.

[8]English Alabaster Carvings as Records of the Medieval Religious Drama (Oxford, 1949).

[9] Drama and Imagery in English Medieval Churches (Cambridge, 1963).

[10] The Production of Medieval Church Music-Drama (Charlottesville, Va., 1972).

[11] L'Art religieux du XIIe siècle en France, 3rd ed. (Paris, 1928), p. 127.

[12] Rice, p. 187; Neil C. Brooks, The Sepulchre of Christ in Art & Liturgy. Illinois Studies in Language & Literature, VII, 2 (May 1921), 1-110.

[13] John Gage, "A Dissertation on St. Ethelwold's Benedictional, an Illuminated Manuscript of the Tenth Century," Archaeologia, XXIV (1832), 1-117.

[14] John Gage, "A Description of a Benedictional, or Pontifical, called 'Benedictionarius Roberti Archiepiscopi', an Illuminated Manuscript of the Tenth Century, in the Public Library at Rouen...," Archaeologia, XXIV (1832) 118-136.

[15] Benedictional of Archbishop Robert, intro.

[16] Rosemary Cramp, "Anglo-Saxon Sculpture of the Reform Period," Tenth-Century Studies, ed. David Parsons (London, 1975), p. 184.

[17] Rice, p. 41.

[18] Rice, p. 81.

[19] Rice, pp. 84-86.

[20] Cramp, p. 199.

[21] Rice, p. 93.

[22] D. M. Wilson, "Tenth-Century Metalwork," Tenth-Century Studies, ed. David Parsons (London, 1975), p. 200.

[23] Rice, p. 250.

[24] Rice, p. 253.

[25] Churches at Deerhurst, Glastonbury, and Canterbury are discussed in H. M. Taylor, "Tenth-Century Church Building in England and on the Continent," Tenth-Century Studies, ed. David Parsons (London, 1975), pp. 141-169.

[26] "Winchester Cathedral in the Tenth Century," Archaeological Journal, XCIV (1957), 28-68.

[27] Quirk, p. 30.

[28] The interim reports of the excavations appeared both in the Winchester Cathedral Record and the Antiquaries Journal, but they have been issued in one volume by Martin Biddle, The Old Minster: Excavations near Winchester Cathedral, 1961-1969 (Winchester, 1970).

[29] Old Minster, p. 4.

[30] Old Minster, p. 11.

[31] Old Minster, p. 47.

[32] Old Minster, p. 47.

[33] Old Minster, p. 51.

[34] Old Minster, p. 51.

[35] Old Minster, p. 93.

[36] Rose Graham, "The Intellectual Influence of English Monasticism between the 10th & the 12th Centuries," Transactions of the Royal Historical Society, New Ser., XVII (1903), 30.

[37] R. N. Quirk, "The Cathedral School a Thousand Years Ago," Winchester Cathedral Record, XXVII (1958), 4-8.

[38]Intro. R.W. Hunt. Umbrae Codicum Occidentalium, No. 4 (Amsterdam, 1961).

[39]Dorothy Whitelock, "The Authorship of the Account of King Edgar's Establishment of the Monasteries," Philological Essays: Studies in Old & Middle English Language & Literature in Honour of Herbert Dean Meritt. Ed. J. L. Rosier (The Hague, 1970), pp. 125-136.

[40]Helmut Gneuss, "The Origin of Standard Old English & AEthelwold's School at Winchester," Anglo-Saxon England I, ed. Peter Clemoes et al. (Cambridge, 1972), p. 69.

[41]Gneuss, p. 83.

[42]"Three Latin Poems from AEthelwold's School at Winchester," Anglo-Saxon England I, ed. Peter Clemoes et al. (Cambridge, 1972), pp. 85-137.

[43]"Late Old English Literature," Tenth-Century Studies, ed. David Parsons, (London, 1975), p. 111.

[44]For much of the discussion of medieval music, I am indebted to Richard H. Hoppin, Medieval Music (New York, 1978), pp. 31-33, passim.

[45]Margaret Deanesly, Sidelights on the Anglo-Saxon Church (London, 1962), p. 75.

[46]Deanesly, pp. 66-74.

[47]Bibliothèque Nationale MS. Lat 987. See New Palaeographical Society, Facsimiles of Ancient Manuscripts, etc., ed. E.M. Tomlin et al. (London, 1903-12), 1st Series, I, pls. 83-84.

[48]The Benedictional of Saint-AEthelwold, Bishop of Winchester 963-984, ed. George F. Warner and H.A. Wilson (Oxford, 1910). The MS. Add. MS. 49598, is in the British Museum.

[49]Alexander, p. 169.

[50]Rice, pp. 194-223.

[51]The Bosworth Psalter, ed. F.A. Gasquet and E. Bishop (London, 1908).

[52]Deansley, p. 84.

[53]Hoppin, p. 144.

[54]Jacques Chailley, L'Ecole Musicale de Saint Martial de Limoges jusqu'à la Fin du XIe Siècle (Paris, 1960).

[55]Hoppin, p. 145.

[56]Hoppin, p. 146.

[57]The Winchester Troper from Manuscripts of the Xth and XIth Centuries, ed. W.H. Frere (London, 1894), intro.

[58]Knowles, p. 60.

[59]The Repertory of Tropes at Winchester (Princeton, 1977), I, 391.

[60]Planchart, p. 392.

[61]John Godfrey, The Church in Anglo-Saxon England (Cambridge, 1962), p. 302.

[62]H.B. Bittermann, "The Organ in the Early Middle Ages," Speculum, IV (1929), 400.

[63]Translated in Willi Apel, "Early History of the Organ," Speculum, XXIII (1948), 206.

CHAPTER V

LITURGICAL MUSIC–DRAMA

Two of the three goals of this book have now been accomplished. The forces that prompted the introduction of the liturgical music-drama having been described, the remainder of these pages is devoted to suggesting ways in which the period of freedom from foreign invasion, the advancement of civilized pursuits, the influence of continental monasticism, and the personalities of the reforming bishops, especially Ethelwold, resulted in the genesis and propagation of cloister drama. In considering these matters, one takes issue with the opinion of Omer Jodogne: "One ought never disagree about its [music-drama's] origins, because they are evident."[1] On the contrary, very little about this subject is evident; most of the prevailing conclusions are conjectural and tentative. All require re-examination.

Authorship of the Visitation to the Sepulchre

Despite the predilections of the literary evolutionists, a work of art must have a creator; it cannot be the result of an impersonal process. A person of genius was necessary to translate existing musical and mimetic materials into drama. One need look no further than to Ethelwold to discover the author of the Latin Easter play. These pages are rife with observations upon which to base this conclusion, but perhaps they should be summarized here. First, Ethelwold is accepted as the principal author of the Monastic Agreement: why deny him the authorship of the play contained therein? Second, as a monastic bishop, he was not cloistered; in the secular world in which he moved, Ethelwold was exposed to whatever influences inspired Christian drama. Third, he had a strong motive for creating an effective tool of didactic instruction: only through education could power over contentious nobles be maintained by the king, and only through monastic learning could civilization be advanced toward these ends. Fourth, churches in Britain traditionally enjoyed a modicum of independence from Rome, and the pope's approval of Ethelwold's activities at Winchester granted him special latitude in dealing with purely English liturgical matters. Fifth, Ethelwold's education and intellectual attainments were prodigious, so he was acquainted through the library with classical antiquity and through emissaries with current trends in Benedictinism. Sixth, his composition of the drama is credible since his reputation as an artist is indisputable and under his aegis the fine arts prospered at Winchester. In isolation, any one of these factors is not sufficient proof of authorship, but taken together, they are more than merely suggestive.

Ethelwold was a man firmly rooted in his own time and place. Ample evidence testifies that England was not a cultural backwater between 955 and 980;

nor was the country politically without stature. Geoffrey Barraclough observes: "By comparison with the situation on the continent of Europe, the achievement of the Anglo-Saxon monarchy in the tenth century was quite outstanding."[2] In view of this fact, there is no reason to assume -- merely because it has been fashionable to do so -- that England was reduced to copying continental models of the religious drama. The English ecclesiastical establishment countenanced a number of innovations -- among them monastic cathedrals, abbot-bishops, and royal patronage of monasticism. Could it not also encompass the introduction of drama by one who was exposed to a number of artistic traditions?

Sources of Ethelwold's Inspiration

Vestiges of classical drama remained in the tenth century, and many instances of exchanging manuscripts among monasteries can be cited. Both L. B. Holland and Charles de Lasteyrie have described the connection among religious houses in the so-called Dark Ages,[3] and it is easy to believe that what was known in one Benedictine abbey was eventually known in all. At least seven tenth-century manuscripts of the plays of Terence have survived, and ancient records refer to others that have been lost. L.W. Jones and C.R. Morey suggest a possible connection between the scriptoria at Winchester and the P MS. of Terence,[4] and they also state that several such manuscripts passed through the copyists' hands at Fleury, where English scribes might have worked with them. "In England, Terence appeared in the catalogues of Peterborough, Durham, Rochester, and Canterbury."[5] Hrosvitha's Terentian dramas could easily have been passed on to Winchester from Gandersheim.

A catalogue of books in the monastic library of Gorze[6] confirms that that Benedictine house had two documents containing Terence's plays. Through Dunstan's contact with Flemish monasticism, Terence's works might have been transmitted to England. The breadth of Ethelwold's acquaintance with literature and his munificence in giving books to his abbeys makes it possible that he knew of Roman drama. The fashioning of classical drama into Christian drama merely required imagination, and perhaps the intermediary inspiration was Byzantine.

The influence of the Eastern Roman Empire on English culture heretofore has been cited repeatedly. Relations between England and Constantinople flourished throughout the early Middle Ages. The discovery of the seventh-century burial ship at Sutton Hoo brought to light a dish with four control marks of Anastasios I (419-518),[7] indicating intercourse between the east and the west, and other records show commerce with England as early as Justinian's reign (527-65). Jack Lindsay concludes, "It seems more than likely then that trade, however sporadic, never ceased along the Atlantic route."[8] Other contacts with Byzantium resulted in the foundation of centers of Greek learning in England, primarily at Canterbury.

Theodore of Tarsus, who became Archbishop of Canterbury in 668, and Hadrian of Africa were sent to reorganize the English church along traditional Roman lines in the mid-seventh century, since the prevailing Celtic church did not recognize the supremacy of the pope. Theodore was well-suited to his task because he

> was a Byzantine gentleman, a Greco-Roman philosopher... who belonged to the old, civilized, learned Byzantine world. He had been imbued... at the school of Athens, with secular and divine letters; he was versed in the old Greco-Roman "artes," and not only in the metrical arts which were a part of rhetoric, but with the mathematical arts, of which so much more was known at Byzantium than in the west....[9]

Until his death in 690, Theodore worked tirelessly to unite the churches in the various English kingdoms, strengthen the episcopacy, establish synodal church government, foster monastic life, and endow Canterbury as a center of literary studies. His crowning achievement was winning recognition as the first archbishop of all the English churches. Hadrian's work complemented that of Theodore, and as a result of their labors, the study of the Greek language was more widespread in Britain than anywhere else west and north of Ravenna, and "even Ireland was outdone as a centre of Greek studies."[10]

The influence of Byzantine culture on that of England continued unabated until the eleventh century, when the Normans pressed their interests with great boldness. Prior to the Conquest, though, currents of Byzantine thought could be detected in several areas of English life. Wilfrid built a Greek-style church with round towers and a central plan at Hexham in the seventh century; such churches then proliferated throughout England. Alfred's church at Athelney minster was X-shaped with rounded ends, and even the initial abbey church at Abingdon (675) had rounded ends, as did the original cathedral at Canterbury. Round towers and apses, features of many Saxon places of worship, are of Byzantine derivation.

In the literary and legal fields as well as the architectural, the Byzantine impetus was felt. The Cheirographia and Greek legal materials were studied at Canterbury alongside the usual canons of Roman law. King Ine of Wessex (688-94) imported Greek scholars to enrich English education. The continuation of Greek studies in England can be seen in the Greek hymn in the Winchester Troper, the Latinized Greek phrases in the Monastic Agreement, and in Saxon art, which has been discussed previously.

Byzantine priest-kingship is emphasized in Dunstan's coronation rite for Edgar, and Ethelwold's placing all the monasteries under the priest-king's control is the logical outcome of that persuasion. Edgar, it will be remembered, styled himself basileos Anglorum in the Byzantine manner; his predecessors had done so occasionally, but with Edgar the practice was habitual.[11]

A few more cursory examples suffice to link the monastic reformers with the Byzantine tradition: (1) the sepulchres depicted in the Benedictionals of St. Ethelwold and Archbishop Robert are in the Byzantine style; (2) the portrayal of figures in illuminations of the Winchester school are classical in essence; (3) Dunstan and Ethelwold met foreign envoys at court, and the records show that Dunstan planned to visit eastern Europe; might this refer to Byzantium? (4) Ethelwold's donation to Peterborough included a Greek book; (5) Dunstan may have journeyed to Rome by way of Ravenna, the center of Greek civilization in the west; and (6) ancient documents show that Hrosvitha, a Benedictine, had been exposed to Greek. [12]

Now it is possible to posit the connection between the creation of drama and the influence of Byzantine/Greek culture on that of England. In the eighteenth century Voltaire suggested in vain that the Western religious drama sprang from a play by Gregory of Nazianze (329-89), who is regarded as the author of The Passion of Christ, written in the style of Euripides. Probably performed in a classical counterpart of readers' theatre, [13] this drama appeared in many European manuscripts, all of which date from later than 1542. Tuilier, a modern editor of the play, believes that there was a European archetypal manuscript as early as the fifth century, [14] so that it would not have been impossible for the drama to have reached England by the tenth century.

That Ethelwold knew The Passion of Christ cannot be proven, nor can it be said with certainty that he was familiar with any of Gregory's works. M.R. James, on the other hand, notes that Gregory's Apologiticus appears in a list of manuscripts of Peterborough Abbey, [15] and translations of the works of Gregory by Rufinius Tyrannius (343-410/11) were widely circulated. The possibility that Ethelwold encountered The Passion of Christ is not so remote as to be dismissed out of hand.

Gregory's drama consists of a prologue and three parts: the Passion and Death of Christ, Christ in the Tomb, and the Resurrection of Christ. Since the Greek and English Easter plays enlarge the biblical account of the Resurrection story, it is not surprising to find similar dialogue. Instead of voicing their grief to the world at large, the Byzantine Marys converse with the Chorus before approaching the garden tomb. Then the Angel, as resplendent "as a sweet, fresh snow, "[16] speaks:

> Fear not, do not be afraid. The one whom you seek is no longer in the grave. The Lord who was crucified days ago is no longer in the grave, he has not remained with the dead. But he has risen and he is abroad in Galilee to make himself known to his disciples, as he said he would. Come near and see: the place is empty. Go therefore, go tell the truth; I have told you everything. Now it is your turn, tell it all to Peter and the rest, that Hell is vanquished and Christ has departed the tomb alive.

Then the loquacious Angel, unlike his more restrained English cousin, continues:

The stone of the sepulchre has been pushed away by force; take care, the guards have abandoned the gates of Hell and are in flight. The dead have thrown themselves upon the ground in invoking the God of light as their Savior; thanks to Him, all the bonds have been shattered.

After this speech Mary the Mother addresses the Angel and the Magdalen. Christ appears soon afterward, and the play moves into what Young calls the third stage.

When considering the many ways in which Byzantine culture was mirrored in England, one wonders how it could have been possible for at least one, perhaps The Passion of Christ, of the hundreds of Greek religious dramas to escape being known in England. All our predilections, though, can make it no more than a possibility, to which must be added another.

Pre-nineteenth-century critics of the religious drama believed that mimes or histriones were connected somehow with the origins of drama.[17] What that connection amounted to is anyone's guess. England was in the mainstream of European civilization in the tenth century, and trade routes linked it with the rest of Europe and the Near East. That itinerant mimes visited England and found there a lucrative reception is not to be doubted.

Historians before and after Allardyce Nicoll have combed existent records to find allusions to mimic activity in Western Europe. Alcuin of York, Charlemagne's adviser, wrote to a friend in 791 that "the man who brings actors and mimes and dancers to his house knows not what a bevy of unclean spirits follows them."[18] That members of the ecclesiastical establishment trafficked with traveling players can be adduced from the many conciliar denunciations of these alliances. The council of Aix-la-Chapelle (816), for example, directs priests and clergy not to witness theatrical performances, as does the Council of Paris (829). Laws of Charlemagne, drafted between 800 and 814, forbid churchmen to keep jesters as part of their households. Nicoll, like Voltaire, has been ignored on the subject of mimic influence on religious drama -- largely because of the lack of precise documentation --, but he should not be dismissed precipitately.

Minstrel activity in England is cited by Alcuin, who had even more to say on the subject: "It is better to please God than the actors; it is better to have a care for the poor than for the mimes.... It is better to feed the poor from your table than the actors."[19] Alcuin, lest it be forgotten, was a priest and abbot; yet he was well-acquainted with the activites of itinerant players, whose travels continued throughout the tenth century.

Dating from the reign of Edgar, a letter from an anonymous English author to Count Arnulf of Flanders, the nobleman who received the exiled Dunstan, has survived. The writer notes that Arnulf's magnificence was "not theatrical like the comedian applauded by the crowd,"[20] but based on the Christian doctrine of charity. Is this not an allusion to current theatrical practice?

97

As a last demonstration of the mimes' presence in England and their corrupting influence on churchmen, a speech of King Edgar, addressed particularly to monks, may be cited. Speaking of the excesses of secular priests, Edgar says:

> I shall say, I will say that the good people mourn, the evil ones scoff. Sorrowing I shall say ... how they [the seculars] wallow in gluttony and drunkenness, in marriage beds and lewdness; so that now the houses of the clerks are considered houses of prostitution, gathering places of actors [author's italics]. There is gambling, there dancing and singing, there even to the middle of the night are extended sessions of shouting and coarseness.... These things the soldiers shout, the people grumble about, the mimes sing and dance about; and you sit by and do nothing.... I have the sword of Constantine, you the sword of Peter in your hands. Let us join right hands... that the sanctuary of the Lord may be cleansed.[21]

In addition to ranking himself as the successor of the first Christian emperor, Edgar was aware of the activities of the performers, who dared to ridicule God's servants in their shows. Can Ethelwold, Edgar's principal adviser and strong enforcer of Edgar's principles, have been ignorant of mimic drama? There is nothing, incidentally, in the king's pronouncement to link the monks with the actors. William Tydeman confuses monks with secular clerks when he says, "Mimi did visit monastic communities, a practice condemned by King Edgar...."[22]

Ethelwold, as a member of the king's council and as a bishop, knew of these excesses excoriated by Edgar, which seem not to have been entirely eradicated by the rigor of the Monastic Revival. Aelred of Rievaulx (1109?-66) in his Mirror of Charity (c. 1142) accused "English priests of using wild theatrical gestures, vocal and facial distortions, dramatic pauses and other practices more suited to the theatre than to the church...."[23] What an ironic historical twist it would be if Ethelwold, determined to expunge secular theatricals from English minsters in the hands of secular clerks, decided to capitalize on his flock's innate mimetic instincts and their fascination with the theatre simply by Christianizing the performances. In conclusion, then, the example of the mimes, classical drama, and Byzantine plays may have been individually miniscule, but their combined effect, galvanized by Ethelwold's reformative resolution and artistic nature, probably spawned the idea of Christian drama. Although the theory of the necessary evolution of the trope into drama is highly questionable, the practice of troping provided the means and occasion of dramatic performance.

The popularity of troping in England is demonstrated by the hundreds of extant tropes of Winchester provenance. Although careless nomenclature has created some confusion as to the precise definition of a trope, "all tropes have one characteristic in common: they expand standard items in the liturgy by the addition of words or music or both."[24] Any general history of music details the development of the trope, described by W.H. Frere as "practically... the sum total of musical advance between the ninth and the twelfth century."[25] It is certain, though, that Ethelwold did not view troping in relation to the usual chant, as Frere does, as "the relation of an abortion to a living organism."[26]

Ethelwold doubtless welcomed troping as a means of further magnifying his Benedictine duty of perfecting the liturgy; as a pragmatist he viewed the trope, not as the source, but as a point of departure for his Christian music-drama. From the Easter Quem Quaeritis trope, already at least fifty years old, he derived the subject matter of his play, the dialogue, and the opportunity and occasion of its performance. What he supplied was a dramatic perspective on the Easter material that replaced its purely narrative aspect. As Wolfgang Michael concludes, "[T]he medieval drama began through an original act well prepared the development of the trope, but an original act after all."[27]

The Visitation to the Sepulchre of the Monastic Agreement

The version of the Visitation to the Sepulchre (hereafter called VS) described in the Monastic Agreement, dating from about 970,[28] is the earliest recorded liturgical music-drama as distinguished from a dramatic trope.[29] Since the conditions of its production suggest that "a considerable dramatic development preceded it,"[30] perhaps the music-drama appeared as early as 950 when Ethelwold was already established as Abbot of Abingdon. Writing of the Easter play, Wright says, "[T]his text probably dates from a period not long after the time when Ethelwold was sending to Corbie for monks to teach reading and singing at the monastery of Abingdon."[31] It is likely, though, that what was brought to England was the latest Cluniac troping practices. Tropes, however, are not drama. The decisive step in transmuting trope to drama occurred at some time between 950 and 970.

Although the primacy of the English "script" [see pp. 2-3] is generally accepted, an examination of other allegedly tenth-century dramas puts Ethelwold's drama in perspective. The VS of St. Vanne of Verdun, for example, is believed to be of the eleventh or an even later century,[32] although scholars from Martene[33] to Young[34] have taken at face value the inscription on the title page of the manuscript, "Saeculo, ut ajunt, X scriptae." Ut ajunt means "as they say" and suggests that the scribe who entitled the document was drawing upon an uncertain tradition that assigned the text to the tenth century. The case for an early date for this play is mitigated further by the novelty of the script.[35]

When the birds have heralded the sunrise, therefore, all the miracles of the resurrection of our Lord Jesus Christ shall be given. As soon as the brethren have heard that, let every one say to himself the verse, Glory be to thee, Lord, who has arisen, etc. Then, after a short time,

all the miracles shall be repeated one by one. Then the cantor dressed
in an archbishop's pall shall stand in the choir, he and two brothers
clothed in white cloaks with hoods are about to sing the invitatory. After
the third response, however, there will be four brothers dressed in
floor-length albs asking by turn, Whom seek ye in the sepulchre, o
Christians? The two others, greeting them, will answer kindly, Jesus
the crucified Nazarene, o heavenly ones. To whom the first Angels will
respond: He is not here; he is risen; go announce.... Those two brothers having heard this shall enter the choir hurriedly with thuribles while
the others perform the verse, and announcing to the empty cross [they
say], The Lord has risen from the grave. Then the abbot, having heard
this, shall begin the Te Deum laudamus, and after having given the
verse, the lauds of matins shall follow, after many lights have been
kindled in the monastery. The antiphon, Yea in the morn, having been
finished, the prayer having been given, let Masses be said.

Whether this ceremony be a drama is debatable. Hardison tries to
discredit Young's view that impersonation is central to drama,[36] but Young is
supported by no less an authority than Aristotle. Hardison rightly maintains
that medieval drama should not be judged by nineteenth- or twentieth-century
standards, but surely the classical view of dramatic art had some vestigial
influence on medieval drama. The essential components of drama -- imitation,
diction, and action in time and space -- may be derived from Aristotle's definition of the theoretically best form of tragedy, and the first and most basic element, imitation, seems to be absent from this rite of Verdun. The rubrics do
not describe the entrance of the Angels or of the Marys. There is no reference
to a tomb except in the lyrics; on the contrary, an empty cross seems to be
the primary spectacular element. The direction that the two brothers enter the
choir hurriedly suggests that they were not originally in the stalls. Where were
they? Possibly at the high altar, perhaps in the nave or crossing. The text is
simply too sketchy and anomalous to be considered the fountainhead of Christian drama, nor were the conditions at St. Vanne particularly conducive to artistic experimentation.

The abbey was founded in 951 by Bishop Beranger,[37] but strict Benedictinism was not enforced until the abbacy of Richard (1004-46),[38] or so a
monk of St. Vanne suggest. Even so, "Verdun never attained a high enough
degree of prosperity or strength for letters and science to be able to win great
distinction there."[39] St. Vanne, consequently, may be eliminated as a possible
home of liturgical music-drama, as well as Toul and Bamberg.

The abbey of St. Evre at Toul was a house of the Fleury connection,
which at first glance might suggest a rapport with Winchester, since delegates
from Fleury participated in the Winchester Synod which ratified the Monastic
Agreement. If the absence of manuscripts of Fleury provenance be evidential,
Fleury had no liturgical music-drama in the tenth century.[40] The monastic
customs of Toul, furthermore, were imported to Verdun by Berenger, who had

100

been a member of the community at Toul. If Berenger as a bishop was unable to institute a drama at Verdun (or was uninterested in doing so), he hardly would have been able to do so at Toul as a mere monk. On the other hand, if Toul had a drama, then Berenger would have been likely to attempt to stage it at Verdun.

Liturgical music-drama at Bamberg is documented by a troper and a gradual, but De Boor maintains that these service books come from Mainz rather than Bamberg. [41] The gradual may be from the late tenth century, but the troper was not completed until 1007. Bamberg (or Mainz), then, cannot be viewed as the home of the VS. For these and other reasons, historians have concluded that Ethelwold's text describes the earliest church music-drama known to have been acted, a novel alternative theory notwithstanding.

In 1903 Bruno Albers argued that since Fleury, St. Vanne, and St. Evre had paschal processions, their rites must be related. He further postulated that since the Monastic Agreement contains Ethelwold's expression of gratitude to Fleury and Ghent, then Fleury must be the home of the VS, whence it spread to Winchester, Verdun, and Toul. [42] Since it cannot be proven that any of these communities, except Winchester, had an Easter play by 975, Albers' conclusions cannot be credited.

In view of these considerations and other recent research, St. Martial of Limoges perhaps ought to be viewed as the home of the Quem Quaeritis trope[43] and England as the home of liturgical music-drama. Until an earlier version of the play comes to light, a remote possibility, the rubrics in the Monastic Agreement must represent the earliest medieval Christian dramatic tradition. Ethelwold either adapted the drama from secular forms or recorded a previously existent play (Hardison's yet-undiscovered prototype) for the spiritual strengthening of English monks and nuns. The facts seem to belie the latter alternative because everything that is known of Ethelwold is characteristic of creative genius, a realization that prompted Wolfgang Michael to conclude that "the authors of the [Monastic Agreement] were the creators of medieval drama."[44] Despite Michael's reluctance to name Ethelwold as the dramatist, his conclusion is wholly consistent with the probabilities established in the preceding pages. Unfortunately documentary evidence may never be forthcoming, so Ethelwold's champions will have to enshroud their arguments in a legalistic nicety:

> When the fact itself cannot be proved, that which comes nearest to the proof of the fact is the proof of the circumstances which necessarily or usually attend such facts, and which are called presumptions and not proofs, for they stand instead of proofs of the fact until the contrary can be proved. [45] [author's italics]

Much has been said about the circumstances leading to the creation of the drama and the identity of its author; the text of the drama itself must now be examined.

Textual study has advanced considerably since the time of Karl Young, and and much enlightening work on the text of the VS of the Monastic Agreement has been published recently. [46] Unfortunately much of it is conflicting, and some of it is confusing. To clarify the issues somewhat, the actual dialogue must be set forth; there is no musical notation in the text, which gives only the first words of the diologized responses.

Most writers have assumed that these indications are merely incipits, or beginnings, of anthems, the full extent of which was known by singers and recorded in various service books. Klapper[47] and Hardison[48] have dissented from this view and seen them merely as abbreviations of well-known scriptural dialogue. Smoldon, a musicologist, shows that these designations belong to a type of service book called an ordinarium, which is concerned with rites and rubrics rather than with words and music. [49] Reconstructing the actual text of the play as performed, then, requires an expansion of the incipits, which Young supplies and which appear here in brackets:

Quem queritis [in sepulchro, o Christicolae]?
Whom seek ye in the sepulchre, o Christians?

Ihesum Nazarenum [crucifixum, o caelicola].
The crucified Nazarene Jesus, o heavenly one.

Non est hic, surrexit sicut predixerat; ite, nuntiate quia surrexit a
    mortuis.
He is not here, he has risen as he predicted; go, announce that he has
    risen from the dead.

Alleluia, resurrexit Dominus, [hodie resurrexit leo fortis, Christus,
    filius Dei].
Alleluia, the Lord has risen, today has risen the strong lion, Christ,
    the son of God.

Venite et videte locum [ubi positus erat Dominus, alleluia].
Come and see the place where the Lord was laid, alleluia.

Surrexit Dominus de sepulchro, [qui pro nobis pependit in ligno, alle-
    luia].
The Lord has risen from the sepulchre, who hung on the cross for us,
    alleluia. 50

Neither Young nor most of his followers made any pretense of relating the dialogue to its musical setting, a deadly oversight, so it is relevant to compare Young's reconstructed text with that of the Winchester Troper, which, it is generally agreed, complements the rubrics of the Monastic Agreement. In each of the following triads, the first line represents Young's expanded text; the second, the Troper Corpus Christi MS. 473; and the third, the Troper Bodleian MS. 775:

Quem queritis [in sepulchro, o Christicolae]?
Quem quaeritis in sepulchro, Christicolae?
Quem quaeritis in sepulchro, Christicolae?

Ihesum Nazarenum [crucifixum, o caecicola].
Ihesum Nazarenum crucifixum, o caelicola.
Ihesum Nazarenum crucifixum, o caelicola.

Non est hic, surrexit sicut predixerat; ite, nuntiate quia surrexit a
    mortuis.
Non est hic, surrexit sicut predixerat; ite, nuntiate quia surrexit,
    dicentes:
Non est hic, surrexit sicut predixerat; ite, nuntiate quia surrexit,
    dicentes:

Alleluia, resurrexit Dominus, [hodie resurrexit leo fortis, Christus,
    filius Dei].
Alleluia, resurrexit Dominus hodie, leo fortis, Christus, filius Dei.
    Deo gratias dicite, eia!
Alleluia, resurrexit Dominus hodie, leo fortis, Christus, filius Dei.
    Deo gratias dicite, eia!

Venite et videte locum [ubi positus erat Dominus, alleluia].
Venite et videte locum ubi positus erat Dominus, alleluia, alleluia.
Venite et videte locum ubi positus erat Dominus, alleluia, alleluia.

----- [This line does not appear in the Monastic Agreement.] -----
Cito euntes, dicite discipulis quia surrexit Dominus, alleluia, alleluia.
Cito euntes, dicite discipulis quia surrexit Dominus, alleluia, alleluia.

Surrexit Dominus de sepulchro, [qui pro nobis pependit in ligno,
    alleluia].
Surrexit Dominus de sepulchro, qui pro nobis pependit in ligno, alleluia.
Surrexit Dominus de sepulchro, qui pro nobis pependit in ligno, alleluia.

The preceding comparisons show that there are some inconsistencies,
notably:

(1) The MA version employs the vocative "o" before Christicolae, while
    neither of the tropers does so.

(2) The MA version contains the phrase a mortuis, while the tropers
    employ dicentes.

(3) The MA text does not contain Cito euntes, as do the tropers.

These sorts of concerns have occupied textual and musicological critics of the
VS. In some cases, clear explanations of textual variations are not forthcoming,
but one example shows the trend. Following the approach of De Boor, several
writers have seen great significance in the appearance of the vocative "o" in the
Angel's address to the Marys. De Boor contends that the presence or absence of

the "o" is due to regional preferences and that families of manuscripts may be identified by its inclusion or exclusion. [51] As a means of clarifying textual relationships, this is a fruitful method. As a means of illuminating conditions of performance though, maintains Smoldon, it is useless, since the "-o" of sepulchro would have been extended so that the effect of o Christicolae would have been achieved. [52] The application of De Boor's theory to Ethelwold's text, moreover, is a moot question because Young's rendering of the "o" in his expansion is wholly arbitrary.

The vocative "o" notwithstanding, there are a number of reasons to link the liturgical conventions of the Monastic Agreement with traditions of Lotharingia and France, chief of which is Ethelwold's statement that representatives from Ghent and Fleury attended the Synod of Winchester:

> ... they summoned monks from St. Benedict's monastery at Fleury and from that eminent monastery which is known by the renowned name of Ghent [St. Peter's Abbey (Blandinium)] ... (Symons, p. 4)

The text itself, moreover, reveals those influences. Hodie resurrexit leo is a French chant, and Venite et videte and pependit in ligno can be traced to Lorraine. De Boor further contends that the antiphon Ite, nuntiate is derived from the oldest north-Italian troping traditions. The English VS is, according to de Boor, zusammengesetzt, "pieced together." [53]

Symons sees more influence from Ghent than from Fleury, [54] while John thinks that the Fleury connection was ascendant. [55] They may all be vindicated by the theory of Guy de Valous, [56] who suggests the following relationship, presented here in translated and simplified form:

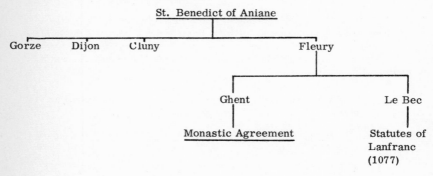

The conclusion, then, is that Ethelwold drew what he liked from previous traditions, filtered it through his imagination, applied it to his specific goals, and created a new thing. The transition from trope to drama was made by Ethelwold, a presumption that must stand until someone demonstrates the contrary.

Propagation of the Easter Play

A word must now be said respecting the ultimate fate of Ethelwold's drama. That it was performed at Winchester under Ethelwold's supervision cannot be doubted, but the acceptance of the production in other English houses is not at all certain. During Ethelwold's lifetime, the VS was probably performed at Abingdon, Thorney, Worcester, Peterborough, Ely, and Glastonbury, [57] and both manuscripts of the Monastic Agreement are of Canterbury provenance and contain the rubrics of the music-drama. Presumably, then, the play was acted by the monks of Canterbury. On the other hand, when the Monastic Agreement was copied for use at Exeter, the section describing the Easter play was omitted, which is somewhat surprising since the abbey at Exeter was a plantation of Glastonbury.

AElfric the Grammarian, Abbot of Eynsham, wrote for his own community a supplement to the Monastic Agreement[58] in which AElfric says his purpose was to place before his monks "some other things which our rule does not touch,"[59] as well as to add liturgical formulas of Amalarius of Metz. The omission of the Easter play from AElfric's treatise has been seen as an indication that the play was not being produced in 1007 (the date of the document). That assumption is unwarranted in view of AElfric's statement that he did not intend to cite everything he had learned at Winchester. In fact, the annual performance of the play probably was traditional by 1007 -- in most of the English houses. It is reasonable to assume that every reformed monastery had a copy of the Monastic Agreement, so why should the play repeatedly be re-transcribed?

The VS was not superseded until the Norman Conquest at the earliest. By the time Archbishop Lanfranc (1005?-89) replaced the Monastic Agreement with his Consuetudines, the liturgical music-drama had spread to Europe and undergone extensive adaptation there. The Normans may have brought a considerably more complex liturgical play to England than Ethelwold's. If the absence of English manuscripts of other music-dramas prior to 1066 be evidentiary, it must be concluded that for some reason the VS fully satisfied the English church's need for drama. Perhaps the growing ferocity of the Viking incursions of the 990's deflected attention from liturgical innovation.

The Music-Drama of the Winchester Troper

As noted above, two musical texts of the VS appear in the Winchester Troper, which should be called a cantatory rather than a troper since it contains several kinds of chants as well as tropes. The musical-dramatic scores outlined under the title The Angel of Christ's Resurrection are not, strictly speaking, tropes, although their music is recognizably that of the Quem Quaeritis trope as sung throughout Europe. [60]

Cambridge, Corpus Christi MS. 473 was written between 996 and 1006, several years after Ethelwold's death, but certainly preserves much traditional material. Oxford, Bodleian MS. 775 is of special significance because it reflects the chant repertory of the Old Minster during Ethelwold's tenure as abbot-bishop; parts of this text date from 978-80. The VS is inscribed in Fol. 26v of CC 473 and in Fol. 17r of Bo 775. Naturally the version of the VS in the Monastic Agreement and those in the Troper are related, Ethelwold himself and his influence being the connecting link. The music and the drama are so interrelated that they seem organically fused.

A reconstructed musical score of the VS appears in the preface of this book, and the verbal text was presented in this chapter (p. 134), so it is possible to embark immediately upon a consideration of some further implications of the troper materials. Musicologists as well as liturgists and philologists have contributed recently to a renewed understanding of music-drama at Winchester. Since the version of the play contained in the Winchester-Troper is the earliest extant example of a music-drama with musical notation and since the musical aspects of the play have suffered from scholarly neglect, it is fair to speak first of those matters.

The music of the VS is, of course, medieval chant of a rather advanced type, which is "exclusively vocal and entirely monophonic."[61] No sort of musical accompaniment, not even that of the great organ in the Old Minster, was required,[62] nor was any sort of harmonic embellishment. Monks were expected to learn the words and music of chants by heart, but the addition of new church music necessitated some sort of notation to jog the singers' recollection of materials already rehearsed and learned. The resultant system for indicating melodic progression involved heighted neumes, or signs, that were written on liturgical texts. The difficulty lay in the fact that neumes were incapable of indicating melodic intervals or even the starting note of a chant. "The notation thus served only as a memory aid for a singer who already knew the melody. For anyone else it was useless."[63]

The type of notation employed by the compilers of the Winchester Troper is cheironomic (literally "hand gestures," referring perhaps to the conducting of the choir director), which originated in Byzantium.[64] The implications of the use of cheironomic notation for students of the music-drama are momentous: one simply cannot precisely reconstruct the music of the VS, "the deciphering of which is extremely dubious, to say the least."[65]

The actual musical text employs two modes, the first line being in Dorian, the remainder in Hypomixolydian.[66] Adopting the names but not the substance of its modes from ancient Greek music, medieval chant moves in any of eight modes, each of which employs a different set of intervallic relationships to define the octave. The Authentic Modes are the Dorian, Phrygian, Lydian, and Mixolydian; the so-called Plagal Modes are related to the others and are named by adding "hypo-" to the authentic from which they are derived.[67] The modes are distinguished by the quality of tonality.[68]

"The music is peaceful and serene," as Dolan remarks, and as in modern music-drama, grows out of and supports the text, which presumably was the standard practice. This integrality of text and music certainly is characteristic of medieval chant, but the absence of any other tenth-century texts of music-drama (with music, that is) precludes any firm conclusion. The music of the Winchester play, on the other hand, does not support the use of an "angelic voice" nor any attempt vocally to portray "the glory of the resurrection."[69] Restraint and dignity seem to be the musical intentions.

A word must now be said about the lyrics of the troper VS. Planchart has catalogued all the Winchester music and concludes that it is of two types: that of English origin and that of continental provenance that replaced earlier English chants. Of the entire repertory, he believes that 168 out of 268 are of French origin, largely from northern France and the Rhineland. There are also concordances with Italian tropes. Lest the English contribution be underestimated, however, Planchart notes:

> Thus the English Tropers also show a large corpus of works that are unique to them, many of which are written in the some times overly elaborate language that we encounter in the language of Wulfstan and other Anglo-Latin poets of the school of St. Aethelwold. Moreover, works clearly taken from continental sources are often rewritten and parodied in ways that bring the final poetic form of the piece quite close to the literary taste of the Anglo-Latin poets.[70]

It seems that Ethelwold's pupils merely followed his example.

A number of discordances between the troper dialogue and that of the Monastic Agreement have been cited (p. 134), some of which have been reconciled by music historians. In addition to Smoldon's solution of the vocative "o" problem,[71] De Boor suggests an explanation of the inclusion of Cito euntes in the troper version of the VS. One might think that the process of expanding liturgical materials was the decisive factor, but De Boor maintains that its use is a reversion to a tradition older than that of the Monastic Agreement.[72] As to the de mortuis/dicentes difference, no satisfactory conclusion is forthcoming.

A much more significant inconsistency between the two texts than any of those mentioned above has to do with the placement of the VS in the daily monastic ritual. Generations of scholars have maintained that the Quem Quaeritis trope was originally part of the Introit Resurrexi of the Easter Mass. They further asseverate that its dramatic potentiality could not be realized in such proximity to the holiest, most inflexible rite of the Church.

When Ethelwold dramatized the Easter trope and moved it to the Third Nocturn of Matins, the most complex of the celebrations of the Canonical Hours, he set the stage for the further development of Christian drama. Freed of the liturgical restrictions of the Mass, Ethelwold employed the more flexible creative opportunities provided by performance at Matins. This, too, is in line with traditional scholarship, but, until recently, no one has explored Ethelwold's reasons for performing the play at Matins. If freedom from liturgical restraint were his primary motivation, why not produce the play wholly independently of the liturgy?

Dom Jude Woerdeman has supplied the answer. In monastic houses the celebration of Matins was a lengthy and complex business; in secular churches, however, where the Roman Rite was observed, Matins was a shorter service, being particularly abbreviated during the Easter season. There was another dissimilarity, though, and one more germane to the music-drama: the monastic ritual of St. Benedict required the reading of the Easter story from the Gospel of St. Mark after the singing of the Te Deum. For the Benedictine, it will be remembered, the Work of God consists primarily in celebrating the liturgy, and doubtless the monks endeavored to render all the Easter services in a particularly resplendent manner. To the monk, the reading of the Gospel was a particularly significant part of the office of Matins, one wholly absent from the Roman Rite.

The reading of the Gospel, as Woerdeman describes it, is not without its theatrical appeal:

> The superior of the monastery, normally an abbot who was a prelate, read or sang the Gospel lesson. Having intoned the Te Deum, he went to the sacristy and donned his sacred vestments. Then in solemn procession he went to the altar. Preceding him were two acolytes, clothed in albs and carrying lighted candles; and two subdeacons and two deacons, the four wearing copes, and the subdeacons carrying censers with burning charcoal and incense. The abbot ascended the altar, kissed it, and took the Gospel book from where it lay on the altar. Then from a kind of pulpit he read the Gospel lesson, probably in a chant tone. On either side of him stood a deacon, and next to the deacon, a subdeacon with a censer. At the conclusion of the Gospel, the choir answered Amen, and immediately the abbot intoned the hymn Te decet laus, and and offered the prayer following it. This being done, he and the ministers retired to the sacristy. [73]

Such ritual doubtless had strong emotive and associative power, yet forces were at work to deprive the monks of the satisfaction of this particular ceremony.

For well over one hundred years, there had been agitation to compel monastic houses to conform to the Roman Rite during the Easter season, a movement that fructified in the Monastic Agreement. Ethelwold, for reasons known only to himself, conceded this point. The concession, though, was a small one because he merely substituted a dramatic representation of the Gospel events for a ceremonial reading of them. It will not have escaped notice that the details of costuming and hand properties are quite similar in the Gospel-reading and the Gospel-acting. The conclusion, then, is that Ethelwold interpolated the play in the Matins service, and not elsewhere, not to escape liturgical restrictions, but to compensate for the loss of such ceremonial.

The problem arises, however, with the realization that the Oxford manuscript of the troper VS, generally a reliable guide to liturgical practices, places the music-drama not at Matins on Easter but at the ceremony of the Blessing of the Paschal Candle, a segment of the Easter Vigil on Holy Saturday, which Ethelwold describes in this manner:

> On Holy Saturday at the hour of None, when the abbot enters the church with the brethren, the new fire shall be brought in, as we said before, and the candle which has been placed before the altar shall be lit from that fire. Then, as is the custom, a deacon shall bless the candle saying, in the manner of one reading, the prayer Exultet iam angelica turba coelorum. Presently, on a higher note, he shall sing Sursam corde and the rest. When the blessing is finished a second candle shall be lit; these two lighted candles being held each by an acolyte, one to the right and the other to the left of the altar.... (Symons, p. 47)

How, then, may this contradiction be resolved? Hardison concludes after extensive examination of texts that the traditional trope-into-drama hypothesis is insupportable, that the VS had a separate development from that of the trope and was from the beginning associated with the Easter Vigil.[74] He has not, however, been able to provide the text of this protodrama that presumably antedated Ethelwold's.

Hardison shattered a number of long-held tenets of the origin of medieval drama, and his dismissal of the troping hypothesis produced fruitful results. Timothy J. McGee studied the relation of the Quem Quaeritis trope to its various liturgical locations and decided that the exchange between the Marys and the Angel was not regarded as a trope at all in a narrow sense [note the title of the VS in the Winchester Troper] and probably underwent a separate and distinctive musical and dramatic development. The troper placement, according to McGee, supports this contention, representing a reversion to older traditions than those of the reformative Monastic Agreement.[75] McGee, too, has not been able to adduce a music-drama that pre-dates Ethelwold's.

Although these observations do not wholly harmonize the discrepancies between the Monastic Agreement and the Winchester Troper, they suggest possibilities that in no way diminish Ethelwold's invention. Hoppin is correct in saying, "The old hypothesis that liturgical drama developed from the process of troping preexistent chants is no longer tenable,"[76] but one must admit that, whatever the process, Ethelwold took the decisive step in transforming rite into drama. His placement of the VS in the Matins observance represents his attempt to display his handiwork in a context that more than compensated for changes wrought by the Monastic Revival.

Notes

1 "Recherches sur les débuts du théâtre religieux en France," Cahiers de Civilisation Médiéval, VIII (1965), 1.

2 The Crucible of Europe: The Ninth & Tenth Centuries in European History (Berkeley, 1976), p. 141.

3 Traffic Ways about France in the Dark Ages, 500-1150 (Allentown, PA., 1919); L'Abbaye de Saint-Martial de Limoges (Paris, 1901), p. 248.

4 The Miniatures of the Manuscripts of Terence ....(Princeton, 1931-32), II, 101.

5 James S. Beddie, "The Ancient Classics in Mediaeval Libraries," Speculum, V (1930), 9. Beddie also shows (p. 13) that Seneca is mentioned in the library lists of Durham, Peterborough, Bury, Reading, and Glastonbury.

6 D.G. Morin, "Le Catalogue des Manuscrits de l'Abbaye de Gorze au XIe Siècle," Revue Bénédictine, XXII (1905), 1-14.

7 R. L. S. Bruce-Mitford, The Sutton Hoo Ship Burial (London, 1968). See Plate XIX for the Anastasios dish.

8 Byzantium into Europe (London, 1952), p. 291. See also Louis Bréhier, "Les Colonies d'Orientaux en Occident," Byzantinische Zeitschrift, XII (1903), 1-39.

9 Margaret Deanesly, The Pre-Conquest Church in England (London, 1963), p. 104.

10 Lindsay, p. 292.

11 Registrum Hamonis Hethe Diocesis Roffensis, A.D. 1319-1352, ed. Charles Johnson. Canterbury and York Series, No. 41 (Oxford, 1948), I, 32-33. Edgar also styled himself (in Latin) "King," "Governor and master," "chief," "emperor augustus," "king and chief," and (in Greek) "ruler."

12 Henricus Bodonis, "De Illustri virgine sanctimoniale coenobii Gandesiani Hrosvita," Scriptorum Brunsuicensia Illustrantium, ed. G.W. Leibnitz (Hanover, 1711), III, 712.

13 Vénétia Cottas, Le Théâtre à Byzance (Paris, 1931), pp. 235-249.

14 Grégoire de Nazianze, La Passion du Christ, trans. André Tuilier. Sources Chrétiennes, No. 149 (Paris, 1969), p. 7.

15 Lists of MSS. Formerly in Peterborough Abbey Library. Supplement to the Bibliographical Society's Transactions, No. 5 (Oxford, 1926), p. 28. Gregory's works were also represented in the library of St. Martial de Limoges. See "Les Manuscrits de Saint-Martial de Limoges," Bulletin de la société Archéologique et Historique du Limousin, XLIII (1895), 54.

16 La Passion du Christ, p. 297.

17 See Hermann Reich, Der Mimus (Berlin, 1903).

18 Quoted in Allardyce Nicoll, Masks, Mimes, and Miracles: Studies in the Popular Theatre (New York, 1963), p. 147.

19 Nicoll, p. 149.

20 Quoted in J. D. A. Ogilvy, "Mimi, Scurrae, Histriones: Entertainers of the Early Middle Ages," Speculum, XXXVIII (1963), 613.

21 Walter de Gray Birch, ed., Cartularium Saxonici (London, 1885-93), III, 573. "... conciliabulum histrionum ... mimi cantant et saltant...."

[22]The Theatre in the Middle Ages: Western European Stage Conditions, c. 800-1576 (Cambridge, 1978), p. 190.

[23]Ibid.

[24]Richard H. Hoppin, Medieval Music (New York, 1978), p. 14.

[25]The Winchester Troper from MSS. of the Xth and XIth Centuries (London, 1894), p. vi.

[26]Frere, p. 5.

[27]"Tradition and Originality in the Medieval Drama in Germany," The Medieval Drama, ed. Sandro Sticca (Albany, 1972), p. 25.

[28]The exact date of the Monastic Agreement cannot accurately be fixed. The range of proposed dates extends from 957 (De Boor) to 975 (Young).

[29]Among the scholars who agree on this point are Axton, De Boor, Dolan, Donovan, Gamer, Hardison, Michael, Smoldon, and Wickham; for their works, see the Bibliography. Also see Edith A. Wright, The Dissemination of the Liturgical Drama in France (Bryn Mawr, 1936), pp. 113-114.

[30]Arnold Williams, The Drama of Medieval England (E. Lansing, 1961), p. 12.

[31]Wright, p. 114.

[32]Usmer Berlière, "Coutumiers Monastiques," Revue Bénédictine, XXIX (1912), 367.

[33]Edmund Martene, De Antiquis Ecclesiae Ritibus, 4 vols. (Antwerp, 1736).

[34]Young, I, 578.

[35]"Consuetudines insignis monasterii Sancti Vitoni Verdunensis," in Martene, IV, 853.

[36]O. B. Hardison, Jr., Christian Rite and Christian Drama in the Middle Ages: Essays in the Origin and Early History of Modern Drama (Baltimore, 1965), pp. 30-32.

[37]H. Dauphin, Le Bienheureux Richard, Abbé de Saint-Vanne de Verdun, 1046. Bibliothèque de la Revue Ecclésiastique, Facs. 24 (Louvain, 1946), passim.

[38]"Gesta Episcoparum Viridunensis auctoribus Bertario et anonymo monachis S. Vitoni," Patrologia Latina, ed. J.-P. Migne (Paris, 1884-1904), CXXXII, 502-528. See Ch. VII, col. 520.

[39]Ministre de l'instruction publique, Catalogue général des Manuscrits de Bibliothèques Publiques de Départements (Paris, 1879), V, 419.

[40]Helmut De Boor, Die Textgeschichte der Lateinischen Osterfeiern (Tübingen, 1967), p. 94. Albers's text of the Consuetudines of Fleury is corrupt, De Boor believes. It is possible, according to De Boor, that the VS does appear in another MS. of Fleury provenance.

[41]P. 80, n. 59.

[42]"Les 'Consuetudines Sigeberti Abbatis'," Revue Bénédictine, XX (1903), 426-427. Gustave Cohen in Le Théâtre français en Belgique au Moyen Age (Bruxelles, 1953), p. 13, uses the prologue of the same document to prove that Ghent is the source of the music-drama.

[43]Jacques Chailley, L'Ecole Musicale de Saint-Martial de Limoges jusqu'à la Fin du XIe Siècle (Paris, 1960), p. 373.

[44]P. 24.

[45]W. A. Jowitt and Clifford Walsh, Dictionary of English Law, 2nd ed. (London, 1977), I, 345.

[46]C. Clifford Flanigan, "The Liturgical Drama & Its Traditions: A Review of Scholarship 1965-1975," Research Opportunities in Renaissance Drama, 18 (1975), 81-102.

[47]"Der Ursprung der Lateinischen Osterfeiern," Zeitschrift für Deutsche Philologie, 50 (1923), 46-58.

[48]Hardison, p. 197.

[49]William L. Smoldon, "The Origins of the Quem Quaeritis and the Easter Sepulchre Music-Drama, as Demonstrated by Their Musical Settings," The Medieval Drama, ed. Sandro Sticca (Albany, 1972), p. 147.

[50]Young, I, 249-250.

[51]P. 41.

[52]Smoldon, p. 143.

[53]P. 91.

[54]P. li.

[55]"The Sources of the English Monastic Reformation," Revue Bénédictine, LXX (1960), 197-203.

[56]Le Monachisme clunisien (Paris, 1935), p. 21.

[57]Symons, p. lvii.

[58]"AElfric's Abridgement of St. AEthelwold's Concordia Regularis," Compotus Rolls of the Obedientiaries of St. Swithun's Priory, ed. G. W. Kitchen (London, 1892), pp. 174-196.

[59]AElfric, p. 175.

[60]C. Clifford Flanigan, "The Liturgical Context of the Quem Queritis Trope," Comparative Drama, 8 (1974), 46.

[61]Hoppin, p. 57.

[62]Alejandro E. Planchart, The Repertory of Tropes at Winchester (Princeton, 1977), I, 53. Planchart notes that some polyphonic music was accompanied by the great organ, but this does not apply to the VS.

[63]Hoppin, p. 59.

[64]Marie Pierik, The Spirit of Gregorian Chant (Boston, 1939), p. 47.

[65]Willi Apel, The Notation of Polyphonic Music 900-1600, 5th ed. (Cambridge, MA., 1953), pp. 208-209.

[66]Diane Dolan, Le Drame liturgique de Pâques en Normandie et en Angleterre au Moyen Age (Paris, 1975), p. 27.

[67]Pierik, p. 42.

[68]Hoppin, p. 64.

[69]Dolan, p. 27.

[70]Planchart, I, 391-392.

[71]For a somewhat different discussion of this problem, see "Melodies of the Medieval Church Dramas and Their Significance," Medieval English Drama: Essays Critical and Contextual, ed. Jerome Taylor and Alan H. Nelson (Chicago, 1972), p. 79, n. 22.

[72]De Boor, p. 91.

[73]"The Source of the Easter Play," Orate Fratres, 20 (1945-46), 265.

[74]Hardison, p. 191.

[75]"The Liturgical Placements of the Quem quaeritis Dialogue," Journal of the American Musicological Society, 29 (1976), 18-19.

[76]Hoppin, p. 178.

112

CHAPTER VI

THE PRODUCTION OF THE <u>VISITATION TO THE SEPULCHRE</u>

Although it is patently impossible to assess the impact of a theatrical production upon an audience unaccustomed to witnessing drama in church, the attempt must be made to reconstruct the conditions that shaped the performance of the <u>VS</u> at Winchester, which would provide clues to its effect elsewhere. Luckily the Old Minster is one of about a dozen medieval churches directly associated with the production of liturgical music-drama which have been subjected to intense archaeological examination, so it is possible to visualize the presentation in its own theatral space. [1]

The theatrical event is comprised of three elements -- the script, the performance, and the audience -- which must be examined in turn if Ethelwold's creation is to be understood. The text of the <u>VS</u> has been discussed in some detail in the previous chapter, but a dramatic analysis is not complete without considering the affective powers of the drama: that is, the response sought by the playwright. Because of the anti-clericalism of some writers and the discomfiture of others in dealing with things of the spirit, this aspect of the music-drama has been sorely neglected. C. Clifford Flanigan notes that "assumptions about the nature and essence of liturgical phenomena will inevitably underlie and shape any thinking about liturgical drama. "[2] Ethelwold unequivocally states that his dramatic purpose was to strengthen faith, but what were his means?

Some theologians have viewed liturgy as the physical enactment of a corpus of beliefs, while a more recent trend has seen liturgy as the result of a community's individual and corporate encounter with God. In this case ritual precedes dogma. "We might, in fact, think of liturgy as a group's endeavor to reactualize those events of mythic history which it perceives as essential to its welfare. "[3] In these terms, what Ethelwold attempted was to merge spiritual time and actual time and to provide his audience an opportunity to partake of the Resurrection and all it implies and to appropriate its significance for itself. [4] His means were the usual components of the theatre enhanced by the traditions and continuity of the Church and the mystical, psychological effects of ornate ritual.

The Script

The performance of the <u>VS</u> must be viewed in the context of the lengthy paschal ritual as outlined in the <u>Monastic Agreement</u> and the Roman Rite; to see it in isolation is to diminish its impact. The special commemorations of Holy Week are rather fully described in the <u>Monastic Agreement</u> and lengthily explicated by Hardison, [5] so at this point it suffices to concentrate on selected items but to note that the ceremonial actually begins on Palm Sunday.

In the dark morning hours of Maundy Thursday, all the lights in the church were extinguished, signifying the snuffing out of the Light of the World, Jesus. After None had been said, the abbot and brethren in the proper vestments went to the door of the church, bearing aloft a serpent-headed staff that accommodated a candle in the snake's mouth. A flint was used to kindle sparks, which were blessed by the abbot and used to light the candle. The sacrist then carried the staff in procession to the choir where one candle was lighted from the new fire, which represented the pillar of fire that guided the Israelites as they wandered in the desert. [This ceremony was repeated on Good Friday and Holy Saturday, when the staff was borne by the dean and the provost on respective days.] Symbolically the monks were linking the creation of light by purely natural means with the creation of the physical world and the Light of the World.

At the hour of None on Good Friday, the abbot and the monks assembled in the church after the celebrants vested themselves. From the ambo the subdeacon read the lesson from Osee 6:1-6:

> In their affliction they will rise early to me: Come, and let us return to the Lord. For he hath taken us, and he will heal us: he will strike and he will cure us. He will revive us after two days; and on the third day he will raise us up, and we shall live in his sight. . . .

Thus the brethren were reminded of their participation in an event that was presaged by the prophets, occurred in the remote past, and was being efficaciously continued in their own lives.

The second lesson from Exodus 12:1-11 contained the story of the paschal lamb's sacrifice in Egypt, and then St. John's Passion story was narrated. When the lector came to John 19:24, at the words, "They divided my garments among them...," two deacons arose "like thieves" and stripped the altar of the cloth upon which the gospel book had rested. [On Easter Sunday the cloth that had shrouded the buried Cross was replaced on the altar, showing that the miracle of the Resurrection was the foundation of the gospel.]

After appropriate prayers and anthems, the draped Cross was stood some distance before the altar, supported on either side by a deacon, who chanted "My people, what have I done to thee?" and was answered by a pair of subdeacons singing in Greek "Holy God," which was answered by the schoolboys (or the school of singers) chanting the same thing in Latin. The deacons then bore the Cross toward the altar, while an acolyte followed with a cushion. After another musical interchange, the deacons unveiled the Cross, turned toward the monks, and sang, "Behold the wood of the Cross. . . ." The abbot at that point rose from his stall and prostrated himself before the Cross and was joined by the junior and senior monks of the right side of the choir. He then repeated the veneration with the novice and schoolboys of the left side, after which the clergy and monastery workers did likewise.

In Chapter V, Section 46 of the Monastic Agreement, Ethelwold refers for the first time to his innovations, a reference that does not immediately precede the rubrics of the drama but comes before the ceremony of the Deposition of the Cross--an important point. Stressing the wholly voluntary nature of the ensuing ceremony, he says, ". . . if anyone should care or think it fit to follow in a becoming manner certain religious men in a practice worthy to be imitated . . . , we have decreed this. . . . " (Symons, p. 44) The bishop proceeds then to describe the "sepulchre, hung about with a curtain" and the use to which it was put.

The deacons who previously carried the Cross came forward and wrapped it in a cloth representing Christ's shroud. After the Cross had been venerated by the community, they bore it, accompanied by suitable chants, from the altar to the place of the sepulchre, where they "buried" it on the cushion as Christ's body was entombed. This service, called the Deposition of the Cross, started at about 2:30 P. M. From the symbolic burial of the Cross until "the night of the Lord's Resurrection, " the tomb was guarded by small groups of chanting and praying monks. While most of the community went about daily tasks, the vigilant guards around the sepulchre and the drone of their prayers would have been a constant reminder of the solemnity of the occasion. It is at this vigil, incidentally, that Hardison believes the VS was first performed. It will be seen from this lengthy description, and more that follows, that the Easter drama in actuality did not begin at Easter Matins; its prologue was enacted days before.

The service of None on Holy Saturday represented a continuation of the events set in motion on Maundy Thursday and Good Friday. The celebration commenced with lighting the paschal candle with the new fire and singing "Let now the heavenly throngs of angels rejoice. . . . "[6] Then another candle was lighted, and each held by an acolyte at either side of the altar. Then followed the reading of four Old Testament lessons and the required prayers. When the master of the singers intoned "Light the candles" on a high note, all the lights in the church were ignited; when the abbot intoned "Glory to God in the highest . . . , " all the bells began to peal, signifying Christ's victory over the grave. After the reading of the epistle and singing of psalms, prayers were offered, the gospel read, and the service soon completed.

On Easter morning at about 3:30, when the bells were rung to call the monks to Matins, the sacrists had already prepared the church for what was to come by restoring the Cross to its place at the high altar (the Elevation of the Cross). Symbolically Christ had risen from the grave before the appearance of the Marys at the garden tomb.

The assembled community chanted and prayed before three lessons were read and followed by three responses; normally there would have been three sets of three lessons, but the Roman Rite which had displaced the monastic usage altered this practice. During the reading of the third lesson, the actors slipped into their "costumes" and stole quietly to their places, the Angel to the sepulchre, the Marys to some unspecified entrance, where they paused awaiting their cue. During the third response of the congregation, the Marys entered and made their way toward the tomb, acting sorrowful and as if they were uncertain of its location. The remainder of the music-drama was played out along the familiar lines, ending, as one often reads, when the Marys laid the grave clothes on the altar, the prior initiated the Te Deum laudamus, and all the bells pealed. At this point sight of the performers is lost because Ethelwold turns his attention to the monastic community. For him, the drama had not been completed.

Perhaps as a means of linking the VS with what remained of the service, Ethelwold required a priest to recite, "The Lord is risen from the grave, who for us hung on the Cross." Then the cantor started the antiphon, "The Lord is reigning...," the two sides of the choir chanting alternately while the scene was dominated by the Cross surmounting the altar. Five psalms were delivered in this manner, and the choir boys were given the duty of singing "The Lord is risen from the grave." The rest of the day, indeed the following six days, were filled with jubilant songs and readings.

In effect, then, the theatrical event was more complex than usually portrayed. Although one is convinced by the arguments that the Deposition and Elevation of the Cross are dramatic but not drama[7] and that the VS is drama, the distinction seems unimportant in terms of the spiritual and even the aesthetic powers of the Easter celebration. Seeing a Wagnerian production at Bayreuth, where even the ambiance of the place is attuned to the performances, can be a far more emotive experience than seeing the same production in a Broadway theatre after a mundane day's work. Such a festal aura surely intensified the production of the music-drama in the Old Minster.

The Performance

In the last quarter of the twentieth century, audiences have become so imaginatively anesthetized by realistic film and television drama that they are sometimes unwilling and often incapable of understanding, much less appreciating, the highly-styled medieval music-drama. Ethelwold knew that art was not life, although he fully understood their relationship. His goal was to illuminate the life of the spirit, not to reflect the details of daily life. His drama transcends time and geography, so the performance of it in the Old Minster mirrored those spiritual concerns.

One wonders, first of all, who the actors were. Although it is impossible to declare with certainty their names, the identities of some of the monks at Winchester are known: Osgar, who had served Ethelwold in so many ways, may have played a role; other participants may have been Foldberht, Frithegar, Ordberht, and Eadric, since the initial performance was staged before they became abbots of their own houses. [8] Elfstan may have been in the group from

Abingdon who formed the original chapter in the Old Minster; and to the list must be added Ethelwold's most distinguished pupil, AElfric the Grammarian. Wulfstan, the cantor of the Old Minster who was instrumental in copying and assembling the Winchester Troper, may also have been a participant. Beyond this, speculation is useless.

A careful reading of the description in the Monastic Agreement of the observances of Holy Week does not shed much light on the identities of the first actors. Ethelwold, as bishop-abbot, had several responsibilities in the ritual but not in the VS proper: as abbot he blessed the new fire, washed the feet of beggars, prayed, chanted, venerated the Cross, served Communion, and blessed the font; as bishop he consecrated the chrism and gave the kiss of peace. The remainder of the responsibilities were assigned to individuals by virtue either of their monastic or priestly ranks. The dean (decanus) and provost (praepositus), after the abbot, the highest-ranking monastic officers, carried the serpent-headed staff to light the paschal candle; the sacrist (aedituus), in charge of all the ceremonial, also bore the serpent-headed staff and effectuated the Elevation of the Cross. The other monastic groups mentioned are the choir (schola cantorum), the chief singer (cantor), and the boys of the monastic school (pueri). All of these people, as well as the brother-monks themselves (fratres) prayed, sang, prostrated themselves, and served as congregation and audience.

Four of the brethren acted in the VS. Perhaps four additional monks served as supernumeraries, the soldiers set to guard Christ's tomb. Groups of brothers had been detailed to maintain the vigil over the sepulchre "by night" (nocte). Since Matins coincided with sunrise, theoretically it was still night-time when the service started. This possibility is supported by the two previously-mentioned benedictionals, each of which depicts four sleeping guards near the grave. The vigilants in Ethelwold's book hold spears, while those in that of Robert of Rouen have none. If the illuminations can be taken as representative of two different traditions of production, an interesting fact emerges. In the first benedictional, one of the watchers is bearded; in the latter two are hirsute. Benedictine monks did not shave daily, but they were not bearded, especially at Eastertide. The Monastic Agreement specifically orders the monks and boys who were able to shave to do so on Friday and Saturday before Easter.

It is clear, however, that those monks who had entered Holy Orders were often the center of attention as they conducted the liturgy. The Monastic Agreement mentions the priest (sacerdos), in this instance probably Ethelwold himself, who served Communion, prayed, and chanted; the deacon (diaconus), who performed the maundy, stripped the altar, displayed the Cross, wrapped and buried the Cross in the tomb, served at the altar, and blessed the paschal candle; the subdeacon (subdiaconus), who read the lesson, chanted, and assisted at the altar, largely by censing. All of these are referred to as ministers (ministri). The final participant was the acolyte (acolitus), who bore the cushion on which the Cross rested, held candles aloft, and served at the altar. Ethelwold clearly implies, though, that the performers of the VS were chosen because of monastic, not priestly, calling.

More central to understanding the Easter music-drama than the cast-list is a consideration of the performance style. The fact that the diction is in Latin, that all the lines were sung rather than spoken, and that all the roles were played by males makes it certain that a realistic approach was not attempted. Several additional factors must be mentioned, which requires reference to the entire Holy Week ceremonial as outlined above and by Hardison.

The acting style of the VS was not drastically different from the manner in which the whole Easter liturgy was conducted; it probably was little more theatrical than what preceded and followed it. From beginning to end, symbolic action is endemic to the ritual, from the generation of the new fire, to the VS, and to all the successive services. The rubrics specify processions, prostrations, venerations, foot-washing, altar-scrubbing, blessings, expunging light, igniting candles, pealing bells, and all sorts of stylized gestures and movements. They constitute, in effect, pantomimic dramatization or spectable in the Aristotelian sense.

Even the allegedly non-dramatic rites were decidedly theatrical. A case in point is the reading of the Gospel narratives of Christ's Passion, which occurred four times during Holy Week. The stories are inherently dramatic, the events moving. Yet is it not enough to say simply that the Gospels were read. The narration was delivered in a kind of chant tone according to an accepted tradition. In the tenth century Christ's words in the gospel books were preceded by a "t", indicating tarde, or slow; this practice evolved so that the speeches of Jesus were read slowly in a low pitch, those of the Jews fast and high-pitched, and those of the Evangelist in a medium voice. [9] Even the Monastic Agreement contains frequent allusions to the manner in which liturgical elements were to be delivered. The point is, merely reading the Gospel is one thing; reading liturgically was quite another highly theatrical, albeit unrealistic, device.

Another example may be cited. At None on Holy Saturday when the paschal candle was kindled for the third time and a deacon chanted, "Let now the heavenly throngs of angels rejoice...," he did not merely mouth the words. By the tenth century it was common for churches to possess elaborately-illuminated Exultet (the Latin incipit of the chant) rolls in which the chant was written. As the deacon sang the words and unrolled the document over the edge of the ambo, the illustrations were visible to the monks and served to augment the content of the chant. Incidentally, the pictures were upside-down for the deacon.

Even as the manner of presentation was highly styled, the other elements of spectacle contributed to the symbolic nature of the performance. Ethelwold specifies the costumes to be worn by the Marys and the Angel, the former wearing copes (cappae) and the celestial visitor in an alb. An ecclesiastical appropriation of the classical tunica alba, the alb reached from the neck to the ankles and had narrow sleeves. Alba means "white," and it is this trait that made it suitable for the Angel. When the risen Christ was transfigured on the Mount of Olives, his garments became as white as snow. The Apocalypse (7:9) describes those surrounding the throng of God as wearing brilliant white apparel. Thus the Angel wore white. In the illustrations of the Easter scene in the benedictionals of St. Ethelwold and Archbishop Robert and the missal of Robert of Jumièges, the Angel has wings. One wonders if this was simply an artistic convention or if the Angel of the VS actually was alate. Winged or not, he held a palm leaf in one hand, and in these three illuminations, his hand is raised in a Byzantine gesture of blessing. The palm frond is shown in all three service books.

Since copes are outer vestments, the Marys would have worn some sort of robe beneath them, probably the dalmatic, which was a secular garment dating from antiquity. The dalmatic was similar to the alb except that it normally had wide sleeves and often was depicted in paintings as somber yellow. According to drawings in the Roman catacombs, women wore white and dull yellow dalmatics. [10] Whereas usage suggested that albs were appropriate to deacons and bishops, the dalmatic was worn by all ranks of clergy. Copes were essentially cloaks and frequently had hoods attached. All three illuminations depict the Marys' hoods raised over their heads. In their hands they carried thuribles, or censers, to use the more common English term, signifying the ointment jars from which they intended to anoint the body of Christ.

The setting of the play is dependent on the architectural features of the Old Minster in general and the nature of the sepulchre in particular. In Chapter IV, Section 46 Ethelwold speaks of a "representation as it were of a sepulchre, hung about with a curtain" (Symons, p. 44), but that translation is not precise. Ethelwold actually says, "Let there be...a certain representation of the sepulchre and [author's italics] a certain covering stretched out in a circle...." The tomb, then, was encircled by a curtain. Many years ago John K. Bonnell reproduced a depiction of a sepulchre within a baldaquin supported by pillars around which a curtain was drawn. [11] As a matter of fact, the original came from a Byzantine church, and its usage was common in Anglo-Saxon England. [12] That Martin Biddle and his team of archaeologists unearthed four foundation stones that described an eight-foot square around the high altar of the Old Minster suggests that Ethelwold's church indeed contained an altar surmounted by a baldaquin standing on four pillars. If the high altar, in itself symbolic of Christ's tomb, served as the sepulchre, it would not have been difficult to install curtains inside the columns that supported the dome. That is one possibility, but there are others.

The rubrics of the VS dictate that the Angel sits at the sepulchre, but they do not specify upon what. In each of the Easter illuminations introduced earlier, the Angel is seated upon a sarcophagus. Perhaps such a structure rested beneath the baldaquin. Alternatively, Bonnell and others have observed that Easter sepulchres frequently were erected over the tombs of saints and holy men. Perhaps the sepulchre was built over St. Swithun's shrine in the western end of the church. [13]

That speculation leads to the theories of Carol Heitz, who has studied the function of west-works[14] in Carolingian churches. Heitz points out that the majority of liturgical dramas originated and were performed in abbey churches that contained west-works.[15] Surely there was a connection, Heitz believes, between west-works and the performance of drama, since it was not obligatory to place sepulchres near the high altar.[16] If not here, where? In the west-works, of course. Ethelwold, however, seems to thwart Heitz's theory; he says the tomb was to be situated "in a part of the altar where there was space." Granted, Ethelwold does not mention the high altar specifically. He could have meant a subsidiary altar, such as that near the site of St. Swithun's grave, just outside the west portal. If the Monastic Agreement were written around 974, he might have referred as well to the new shrine of St. Swithun which stood immediately east of the high altar. So where in the Old Minster was the sepulchre situated? That is a very important question because the blocking of the play depends on the answer, one that cannot be posited without noting some essential dimensions of the abbey church of SS. Peter and Paul in the Old Minster:

(1) At the extreme western end of the church complex lay St. Martin's Tower, approximately 25' x 40'.

(2) St. Martin's Tower was separated from the west portal of the church by c. 65'.

At some time between 974 and 980, that intervening area was filled by the erection of the gigantic apsidal construction that focused on the shrine of St. Swithun and accommodated many pilgrims. At the same time an aditional shrine of St. Swithun was built east of the high altar.

(3) From the front of the high altar to the front of St. Swinthun's western shrine was c. 90'.
Around 980 the apsidal construction was abandoned and the west-works built.

(4) From the front of the high altar to the front of the west-works was c. 30'.

(5) From the front of the high altar to the west portal was c. 70'.

(6) From the west portal to the western side of the crossing was c. 40'.

(7) Although the nave was not perfectly rectangular, it was c. 24' wide.

(8) The entire complex, from St. Martin's Tower to St. Swithun's eastern shrine was c. 200' long.

With the ground-plan of the church and its dimensions laid out, it seems that two possible locations of the sepulchre emerge, both of which lie along the west-east axis of the church: the western shrine of St. Swithun and the high altar area. If the sepulchre were on or near St. Swithun's shrine, the monks faced west to view the drama; if it were near the high altar, they faced east. Perhaps the Marys entered from the end opposite to the sepulchre. The matter of the west-works need not enter this discussion since the drama antedated that construction. One argument in favor of locating the sepulchre near Swithun's shrine is that that area was open to the public at large. A lay congregation could have watched from there.

On the other hand, Ethelwold's directions must not be taken too lightly; one thinks that he would have stipulated the use of a subsidiary altar if he had so intended. So a suitable eastern location of the tomb must be found, a task fulfilled by Biddle and his associates. Approximately fourteen feet west of the high altar and on the west-east axis, they located a foundation stone of another altar or tomb. This is a likely place for the sepulchre, especially in view of the location of the choir stalls.

The Monastic Agreement notes the existence of stalls on the left and right of the choir, but where were they? The front of the high altar and the eastern side of the crossing lay on the same line, leaving only twenty feet in the crossing for the stalls. Allowing two rows of two-foot-wide stalls on either side accommodates only twenty monks and children. The community was considerably larger than this. A single row of twenty two-foot stalls on either side of the nave would provide space for forty monks; double rows would accommodate eighty. This means that the sepulchre sat two feet west of the western side of the crossing and divided the space between the high altar and the eastern-most choir stalls. When the Marys entered from the west portal, they filed between the rows of monks (single rows of stalls would leave an aisle eighteen feet wide; double rows, a twelve-foot gangway) as they made their way toward the sepulchre. Then the stage directions for the Marys to turn from the Angel to the choir make sense, as does the Angel's calling them back from the choir to the sepulchre.

Aside from the hand-properties of the Angel and the Marys, the only other object mentioned in the VS is the winding cloth. When it is first mentioned in the Deposition, Ethelwold says that the Cross was wrapped in fine cotton or muslin (sindone). When the Marys display the wrappings to the congregation during the VS, Ethelwold uses lintamina, or "linens." Presumably the linens rested upon the cushion that had been laid in the tomb at the Deposition.

The Audience

That the VS was intended as an awe-inspiring, didactic experience is unquestioned, but historians have not been careful properly to identify the recipients of its teaching. Chambers is probably guilty of initiating the confusion because of what he leaves unsaid, writing that the purpose of music-drama was "devotion and edification."[17] Writers such as Craig and Nicoll perpetuate the belief that the drama was initially intended for the crude and unlettered commonality. According to Hardin Craig, "The medieval religious drama existed primarily to give religious instruction, establish faith, and encourage piety. "[18] The statement is true enough, like Chambers before him, Craig fails to mention for whom the religious theatre was established, so it has been assumed that the Winchester audience was composed of a lay congregation. Allardyce Nicoll writes, "Finding its basis in the symbolic nature of the service of the Mass, drama developed out of the desire on the part of the clergy to place the salient facts of Christ's life before their congregations. "[19] Clearly, Nicoll means a lay congregation. These historians and others have perpetuated a misconception because they all disregarded Chambers' own admonition to study the environment in which an art-form is produced (see the title page).

If the music-drama were presented to teach vulgar folk, they must have been present at its performance. If, however, it can be argued that the audience was composed of people other than the parish constituency, then the prevalent opinion about the audience must be changed.

The Monastic Agreement is not a long document, so it is not difficult to extract the types of people discussed therein: the monks and their officers (fratres, priores, abbates, seniores, juniores, aeditui, decani, episcopi, presbyterii); the celebrants at the altar (sacerdotes, diaconi, subdiaconi, ministri, acoliti, thuriferi, cantores, schola, hebdomarii); the school children (schola, pueri, infantes); and those who were dependent upon the monastery either for charity or hospitality (pauperi, peregrini, famuli). From these allusions, the population of the Old Minster may be deduced. The primary cenobites were the monks (fratres) and the lay brothers (famuli), who did most of the manual work. There were those men who aspired to the priesthood and had been newly baptized (neophyti). In addition there were the students, who supplied most of the recruits for the monastic calling. In fact, these students lived as monks and participated in the daily regimen. Finally, there were the many poor people who were supported by the monks, as well as a steady influx of pilgrims (peregrini) who had come to share in the miracles of St. Swithun. These, then, are the people to whom the Monastic Agreement refers, and these are the audience of the music-drama.

There are, however, in the Monastic Agreement several statements which at first glance suggest that the laity were admitted to the monastic services:

(1) Ch. I, 23   Mox signorum motu fidelem aduocantes plebem missam incohent. (Symons, p. 19)
(The bells shall ring to call the faithful together and the Mass shall be begun.)

(2) Ch. IV, 40   ... pauperibus ante ad hoc collectis secundum numerum quem abbas praeuiderit.... (Symons, p. 39)
(...there shall be assembled as many poor men as the abbot shall have provided for....)

(3) Ch. IV, 41   ...communicatio praebetur tam fratribus quam cunctis fidelibus.... (Symons, p. 40)

122

(. . . Communion shall be given to all the brethren and to all the faithful. . . .)

(4) Ch. IV, 45 . . . dum omnis clerus et populus hoc idem faciat. (Symons, p. 44)
(. . . until all the clergy and people have done in like manner.)

(5) Ch. IV, 46 . . . imitabilem ad fidem indocti uulgi ac neophytorum corroborundum. . . (Symons, p. 44)
(. . . for the strengthening of the faith of unlearned common persons and neophytes. . . .)

In the first citation, the use of the word plebem, which means the common people in classical Latin, is the basis of the confusion. In this context no difficulty exists if it be remembered that the people are the lay brothers and guests of the monastery. If this argument should not persuade, however, it is useful to recall that lay-folk were freely admitted to the apsidal construction that housed St. Swithun's western shrine. As a final alternative, Ethelwold might have employed fidelem plebem to indicate "the faithful people," the monks themselves. The paupers cited in the second statement did not assemble in the church, but in a suitable place (in locum congruum).

In the instance of the third statement, Symons' translation is misleading. The Latin actually says, "Communion shall be given to the brothers insofar as they are all faithful," which might be a reference to the enforced regularity of some of the seculars.

The fourth ceremony concerns the ceremony of the new fire in which the abbot venerated the cross and then returned to his seat and waited until the "clergy and people" had done likewise. "Clergy" in this case refers to the officiants at the altar, and the "people" are the remainder of the community who comprise the congregation.

The key to the identity of the audience of the VS rests in the phrase indocti uuli ac neophytorum of the fifth statement and lends itself to a philological solution. By the time of Augustine (354-430), the word uulgaris was used substantively to denote the "common man." This was employed in preference to the classical Latin uulgus, which means the same thing. The use of the substantive adjective uulgaris was in vogue by 430[20] and continued to be used as late as the twelfth century. [21] It is reasonable to assume, therefore, that Ethelwold realized a difference between the two words and meant something special when he used uulgus in the Monastic Agreement. By Ethelwold's day uulgus had assumed an adjectival meaning and was interpreted to mean "inordinate," "confused," or "incondite." [22] In the statement in question, consequently, uulgi probably means "confused" or "uncatechized" people. Indocti simply means "uninstructed." The meaning of neophytorum has been mentioned earlier; it refers to would-be prelates who had been baptized recently or to oblates espousing monkhood. Ac means "and" in the sense of "and in particular" or "and indeed." On the basis of this reasoning, the phrase may be reconstructed:

> ... for the strengthening of the faith of the confused and uninstructed people (the monks, the novices, the schoolboys) and the would-be priests in particular (in whom was vested the educational mission of the Monastic Revival).

This reading, unlike the traditional one, is wholly consistent with the history of the period.

In summation, then, it is probable that the earliest music-drama was not presented for the edification of the laity, a conclusion based on the following reasons:

(1) The very idea of Benedictine monasticism is opposed to confraternity between cenobites and laity.

(2) The text of the Monastic Agreement nowhere indisputably mentions lay attendance at monastic services in the convent. When lay participation was desired, the monks journeyed to parish churches. [23]

(3) In the tenth century, training the clergy was a far more immediate problem than the instruction of the masses, which followed in due course.

(4) The entire Monastic Revival was an extension of Ethelwold's desire for an educated clergy who, in turn, could precipitate a literate population, especially in spiritual matters.

Hardison is correct in thinking that "all evidence points to the fact that the Regularis sequence is intended for monastic worship and that few, if any, 'unlearned common persons' are expected to participate."[24] Glynne Wickham lends his considerable authority to this conclusion by commenting that the VS "clearly cannot have been a teaching exercise. Had that been the intention, a simple, spoken vernacular text would have been used, and parish churches chosen for the performance of them."[25] That is precisely what happened once the music-drama was removed from the monasteries and performed under secular conditions.

Conclusion

The events that transpired in tenth-century Winchester are unique; their ramifications in the realms of art, ecclesiology, music, liturgics, and polity are enormous. The tenth century, observes Eleanor S. Duckett, commenced in frozen winter, which was relieved in the 920's by the spring of renewed life.

The fruits and flowers of glorious summer appeared in the 960's and resulted in an impressive harvest.

> Constantly, malicious forces interrupted and barred the path of progress; but ever the warring of good against evil went on. As there were pagan invaders, rebel citizens, a multitude of uncultured men, unworthy rulers in Church and state, so were there emperors striving to bring their people into peace and harmony, bishops caring as true fathers for those in their charge, missionaries boldly facing martyrdom, scholars eager to teach and to learn. That the summer of vision was broken by storms does not destroy its truth. [26]

This is the story related in Chapters I-IV of this book in an attempt to actualize E.K. Chambers's admonition that appears on the title page of this book.

English music-drama can be understood only in this context, the analysis of which comprises Chapters V-VI and lends itself to summarization. The creator of medieval music drama was Ethelwold, Bishop of Winchester, who at some time between 950 and 970 formulated the earliest version of the Visitation to the Sepulchre as described in the Monastic Agreement and augmented by the Winchester Troper. Drawing from secular dramatic traditions and continental liturgical practices, Ethelwold fabricated the Easter play, set it within an elaborate, highly theatrical liturgical context, and presented it to the English monastic community as an act of worship. To study the Visitation in isolation from its liturgical setting is to diminish its dramatic magnitude and its powers of exciting awe and admiration of the transcendant reality of the Resurrection in contemporary life.

Notes

[1]Dunbar H. Ogden, "The Use of Architectural Space in Medieval Music-Drama," Comparative Drama, 8 (1974), 63.

[2]"The Roman Rite and the Origins of the Liturgical Drama," University of Toronto Quarterly, 43 (1974), 264.

[3]Ibid.

[4]Blandine-Dominique Berger, Le Drame Liturgique de Pâques: Liturgie et Théâtre (Paris, 1976), pp. 217-221.

[5]Pp. 111-177.

[6]Hardison, p. 147.

[7]Solange Corbin, La Déposition liturgique du Christ au vendredi saint: sa place dans l'histoire des rites et du théâtre religieux (Paris, 1960), p. 95.

[8]See Walter de Gray Birch, ed., Liber Vitae: Register and Martyrology of New Minster and Hyde Abbey, Winchester. Hampshire Record Society, No. 5 (London, 1892), p. 22 for names of brothers of the Old Minster who were prayed for by the monks of New Minster.

[9] Willi Apel, Gregorian Chant (Bloomington, Ind., 1958), p. 207.

[10] F. Cabrol and H. Leclercq, Dictionnaire d'Archéologie Chrétienne et de Liturgie (Paris, 1953), IV, 111-119; XV, 3001-3002.

[11] "The Easter Sepulchrum in Its Relations to the Architecture of the High Altar," PMLA, 31 (1916), 692.

[12] Gilbert Scott, Essay on the History of English Church Architecture (London, 1881). Cited by Bonnell.

[13] This is more than idle speculation in view of the discovery that some Carolingian sepulchres were located in chapels on church porches outside the west portal called "Galilees." See Elie Konigson, L'Espace Théâtral Médiéval (Paris, 1975), pp. 24, 29, 32, 51.

[14] See p. 100 for a discussion of the west-works of the Old Minster. It should be noted, though, that the VS was initially staged before the west-works were added to Ethelwold's church.

[15] Recherches sur les Rapports entre Architecture et Liturgie à l'époque carolingienne. Bibliothèque Générale de l'Ecole Pratique des Hautes Etudes, VIe Section (Paris, 1963), p. 202.

[16] Heitz, p. 181.

[17] The Mediaeval Stage (London, 1903), II, 69.

[18] English Religious Drama of the Middle Ages (Oxford, 1955), p. 15.

[19] The Development of the Theatre (New York, 1958), p. 63.

[20] Henri Chirat, Dictionnaire Latin-Français des Auteurs Chrétiens (Strasbourg, 1954), p. 863.

[21] J. H. Baxter and Charles Johnson, Medieval Latin Word-Lists from British and Irish Sources (Oxford, 1947), p. 460.

[22] Domino DuCange, Glossarium Mediae et Infimae Latinitatis (Paris, 1938), VIII, 395.

[23] Note the location of parish churches in the drawing in Martin Biddle, "Felix Urbs Winthonia: Winchester in the Age of Monastic Reform," Tenth-Century Studies, ed. David Parsons (London, 1975), p. 129.

[24] Hardison, p. 196.

[25] Shakespeare's Dramatic Heritage (London, 1969), pp. 7-8.

[26] Death and Life in the Tenth Century (Ann Arbor, 1967), p. vii.

APPENDIX I

THE HISTORIOGRAPHY OF MUSIC-DRAMA

In a discussion of the origin of tragedy, Gerald F. Else suggests that perhaps the difficulty of proving the traditional theory lies in the fact that "...we have been looking for the clue in the wrong place."[1] The history of scholarship in the area of medieval music-drama, especially that of the late nineteenth- through mid-twentieth century, is a graphic demonstration of similar misplaced emphasis and concomitant unsatisfactory results.

Much of the present difficulty in delineating the genesis of medieval religious theatre can be traced indirectly to the "Father of Art History," Johann J. Winckelmann (1717-68), whose innovative ideas obtained great currency through Lessing[2] and Goethe.[3] In numerous essays and in his monumental History of Ancient Art (1764),[4] Winckelmann shows how art is subject to cyclic growth and decline, passing through four distinct periods. Art at first, says Winckelmann, is primitive and pure, unsophisticated but possessing elemental power. As artists learn effectively to manipulate their media, art objects become simple yet grand, comparable to the refinement of a Doric column. From that stage art becomes graceful and charming, as elegant as the Ionic order. Decline and decay are the results of the fourth period in which hacks and imitators debase former achievements. With respect to this cyclic development, Winckelmann's observations anticipated the theories of organic growth postulated a century later by the literary apostles of Spencer and Darwin. Not limited to the plastic arts, Winckelmann's influence spread to literature as well; Mme de Staël believed that his contributions to literature surpassed his legacy to art history.[5] Winckelmann, thus, may be viewed as a forerunner of literary evolutionism. As scholars began to apply Winckelmann's notions to their study of medieval drama, the foundations of modern criticism in this area were laid.

Although historians of the eighteenth century did not as a rule relate medieval drama and the liturgy of the Roman Catholic Church, Fontenelle noted in 1742 that "they did not simply celebrate the feasts in most of our churches, they acted them."[6] This connection was later echoed by Gervais, Abbot of La Rue in 1834.[7] Critics of the interim period, however, were reluctant to explore liturgy as the seedbed of drama. Credit for popularizing this theory goes to Charles Magnin (1793-1862), author of The Origins of the Modern Theatre (1838).[8] Magnin saw a simple analogy between the lyrical, ritualistic genesis of Greek tragedy and the similar origin of medieval drama. Soon after Magnin's articles and lectures were digested, countless liturgies, early plays, and comparisons between the two were published.

Pre-Darwinist historians were interested in the conditions that led to the creation of medieval drama, an avenue of exploration that was almost abandoned in the wake of evolutionary criticism. One of Magnin's followers, Edélstand Pontas du Meril perspicaciously noted in The Latin Origins of the Modern Theatre (1849): "To evaluate the drama of the Middle Ages... it is necessary... to replace it in the milieu of the circumstances which restrained or favored its development."[9] Unhappily du Meril's admonition was thereafter voiced frequently but seldom pursued.

In the middle of the nineteenth century, the expression "liturgical drama" seems to have appeared for the first time. Between 1849 and 1855 F. Clément published several articles entitled "The Liturgical Drama in the Middle Ages" in Annales d'Archéologie. Soon afterward Edouard de Coussemaker commented in Liturgical Dramas of the Middle Ages (1860)[10] on the scholarly lapses of his predecessors:

> ...but their publications which reproduce the dramatic pieces are incomplete; there is a regrettable omission. The editors have despoiled them of the music which accompanied them, and which is an integral and substantial part of them....[11]

Coussemaker's warning fell on deaf ears, though, because it was not until a century later that the music of the liturgical drama was studied seriously.

After inditing a thesis entitled "Scenic Practices in the Liturgical Dramas and Mysteries of the Middle Ages," Marius Sepet (1845-1925) published The Prophets of Christ (1867).[12] Influenced not only by the liturgical renaissance that emanated from the Benedictine abbey of Solesmes but also by the latest modes of Darwinian criticism, Sepet posed a provocative question:

> Is it possible to prove... that by a series of logical developments, the offices transform themselves into dramas less and less liturgical, until the day comes when mystery and liturgy are not synonymous terms: in a word, that the theatre of the Middle Ages issued from the religion of the Middle Ages in the same fashion and following the same laws as did the ancient theatre in issuing from the ancient religion?"[13]

Sepet's answer is "Yes!" and he shows how liturgical drama developed from the pseudo-Augustinian Sermon against Jews, Pagans, and Arians according to scientific "laws."

In 1878 Sepet published The Christian Drama in the Middle Ages[14] in which he says, "The drama tended to develop itself, to expand itself, and in enlarging, to separate itself from that liturgy which had given it birth...."[15] The organic hypothesis of literary development is fully articulated here. Dramatic art was given birth by its "mother," the liturgy, and, once alive, passed through a series of self-induced mutations which led it to a progressively more complex form. Sepet's theories matured over the years, and in The Catholic Origins of the Theatre (1904)[16] he explores the source of drama, which to him "was the whole complex of dialogued lections and responsories in the Matins office...."[17] In this work Sepet was especially interested in the voice structure of Carolingian chants, in which he saw eminently theatrical qualities. Here is another seminal idea that was ignored in its author's day but highly instructive in view of recent scholarship. His earlier work in particular was so persuasive that adherents were made of Louis Petit de Julleville (1841-1900), Wilhelm Creizenach (1851-1919), and Edmund K. Chambers (1866-1954).

Petit de Julleville related the liturgical drama to the trope,[18] and Creizenach called attention to the fact that the Monastic Agreement and its drama were connected with English monasticism.[19] With these conclusions in mind, Chambers, also influenced by the cultural anthropology of the Cambridge school, became an ardent folk historian, and in his incalculably influential book The Mediaeval Stage (1903),[20] pointed the direction taken by subsequent scholarship until the 1960's.

Chambers was "a far-ranging, deeply learned scholar, exemplary of all that is best in the English tradition,"[21] but his pre-occupation with the organic hypothesis led him and subsequently others in relatively unproductive directions. His influence is fully discussed by Hardison, so it suffices to observe that although current scholarship must take Chambers's views into account, his conclusions must be evaluated in terms of his predilections. Chambers's reputation as a historian of medieval theatre seems somewhat ironic in view of his own admission that a projected study of Shakespeare convinced him that he ought to know something of Shakespeare's dramatic predecessors. That impetus resulted in The Mediaeval Stage, and anthologizers of medieval drama joined him in studying these early works not for their intrinsic merit but as precursors of Shakespeare. John M. Manly, thus, published Specimens of the Pre-Shakesperean Drama (1897),[22] and Joseph Q. Adams later brought out Chief Pre-Shakespearean Dramas (1924).[23]

Between Edmund Chambers and Karl Young (1879-1943), there yawns a critical gulf as wide as a generation. Young's The Drama of the Medieval Church (1933) is the foundation upon which rest all subsequent studies of music-drama, superseding even Chambers. Expressing his debt to Magnin, Sepet, and Petit de Julleville, Young collected hundreds of texts of tropes and dramas and devoted two great volumes to explicating his theory that dramas organically evolved from the simplest trope to the most complex drama.[24]

Chambers, Young, and the evolutionary hypothesis have not been without detractors. Oscar Cargill maintains in Drama and Liturgy (1930)[25] that the influence of secular entertainers tainted the practice of troping, which resulted in Christian drama. By no means original, this theory was put forth by the English antiquarian Thomas Warton (1728-90), who maintained that monks and minstrels were closely associated, even to the extent of monks' writing plays for the minstrels to perform.[26] William Godwin (1756-1836) described their relationship thus:

The clergy were not content with abusing the minstrels, treating them
with the utmost costumely, and refusing them the sacred communion
and Christian burial; they desired... to rival them in their own arts.
They wished to take away from the laity the very inclination to listen to
them; and for this purpose they could think of no better expedient than
to copy their amusements.... [27]

While the earlier writers did not specifically mention the trope, their arguments
were not essentially different from Cargill's. Although all these theories have
been disregarded because of the lack of evidence, they ring true.

Benjamin Hunningher's The Origin of the Theatre (1955) demonstrates
that drama in all ages developed from an innate mimetic instinct and that medieval theatre represents the church's attempt to Christianize pagan rites. According to Hunningher, the authorities decided that "if the word alone could not win,
then the act would be a powerful ally. So it happened that theatre was not reborn
in the church, but was adopted and taken in by her...." [28] Like Cargill's study,
Hunningher's suffers from a lack of proof but has much to commend it as an
operable theory. Unfortunately the supplantation of the evolutionary hypothesis
still lay in the future, but in the interim, some interesting studies were published.

Accepting the general view that liturgical drama was a French creation,
Maria Sofia de Vito in L'origine de Drama liturgico (1938) [29] is the only critic
known to this writer who has resurrected Voltaire's suggestion about a possible
Byzantine influence on music-drama. Grace Frank in The Medieval French Drama (1954) [30] admits that England was the home of liturgical drama, which was,
nevertheless, copied from French sources. Hardin Craig's English Religious
Drama of the Middle Ages (1955) [31] seems a logical extension of Young's work,
but in his scant paragraphs devoted to the origin of music-drama, Craig ex-
presses allegiance to a principle espoused by John M. Manly: each of the three
genres of medieval drama was the product of a period of great intellectual and
artistic activity. [32] Manly was correct, but Craig cites him in vain, for he never discusses those creative impulses in relation to the Winchester music-drama. He offers nothing to shed light on the conditions that engendered the appearance of religious drama in England. Although Richard B. Donovan's primary
interest is Spain, he recognizes in The Liturgical Drama in Medieval Spain
(1958) [33] that the origin of English drama has by no means been delineated satisfactorily. Donovan believes that the material contained in the preface of the
Monastic Agreement is insufficient proof upon which to base the assumption that
the English monks copied continental drama.

Twentieth-century scholarship in music-drama has spawned three titans:
Chambers, Young, and O. B. Hardison, Jr. Chambers and Young shackled students of medieval drama in the toils of the evolutionary hypothesis, an unrelieved
bondage until Hardison's Christian Rite and Christian Drama in the Middle Ages
(1965) appeared. Because of the influence of this collection of essays, particular-

ly "Darwin, Mutations, and the Origin of Medieval Drama," few supporters of the evolutionary hypothesis can be found. In addition to performing this valuable service, a number of Hardison's contentions have provoked productive discussion. Hardison believes that the liturgy of the Roman Church, especially the Mass, is inherently dramatic; to see the Visitation to the Sepulchre as a dramatic oasis in an otherwise arid liturgical terrain is a gross misconception. Young's thesis that impersonation is requisite to drama is also questioned. Perhaps Hardison's most characteristic conclusion is that drama grew out of the Easter Vigil rather than the office of Matins and was not associated with troping at all, having a separate and distinct development. Although Hardison's views have not been accepted in all quarters, his work has been a goad to scholarship in the area of liturgical history and criticism.

Since 1965 more intensive scholarship has been focused on the medieval drama than in any other period since its origin. In two exhaustive bibliographical essays,[34] C. Clifford Flanigan, "saw aspects of the texts which had always been there but had been overlooked."[35] As a result, textual critics have been able to posit persuasive theories on the origin and dissemination of liturgical ceremonies. Musicologists have demonstrated that liturgical drama is music-drama; as a result the musical notation of the plays is for the first time receiving the same attention as the literary texts. The old dichotomy between actual drama and the merely dramatic is being examined and redefined, which has necessitated relating the dramas to their liturgical environments. The theatre historian has allied himself at last with the liturgiologist, the musicologist, and the textual critic and is coming to an understanding of music-drama that is markedly at variance with the traditional notions. Significant progress toward comprehending the actual nature of music-drama has been made since 1964, but much work must still be done. Casting off the misleading predilections of more than a century is not effortlessly effectuated.

Notes

[1]"The Origin of ΤΡΑΓΩΙΔΙΑ, " Hermes: Zeitschrift für Klassische Philologie, LXXXV (1957), 17.
[2]G. E. Lessing, Laocoön; Nathan the Wise; and Minna von Barnhelm, trans. W. A. Steel (London, 1959). Winckelmann's discussion of the celebrated sculpted group, the Laocoön, inspired Lessing's essay.
[3]J. W. von Goethe, "Winckelmann und sein Jahrhundert," Schriften zur Kunst in Gedenkausgabe der Werke, Briefe und Gespräche (Zürich, 1954), XIII, 407-450.
[4]History of Ancient Art, 2 vols. Trans G. Henry Lodge (Boston, 1872).
[5]Mme de Stael-Holstein, De l'Allemagne, 3rd ed. (Paris, 1815), I, 229.
[6]Bernard le Bovier de Fontenelle, OEuvres (Paris, 1742), II, 23.
[7]Essais historiques sur les bardes, les jongleurs, et le trouvières normands et anglo-normands (Caen, 1834), I, 181.

[8] Paris, 1838.

[9] Les Origines latines tu théâtre moderne (Paris, 1897), p. 1.

[10] Drames liturgiques du moyen âge (Rennes, 1860).

[11] Pp. vi-vii. Translated in William L. Smoldon, "The Origins of the Quem Quaeritis and the Easter Sepulchre Music-Drama, as Demonstrated by Their Musical Settings," The Medieval Drama, ed. Sandro Sticca (Albany, 1972), p. 123.

[12] Les Prophètes du Christ (Paris, 1867).

[13] Trans. in Oscar Cargill, Drama & Liturgy, (New York, 1930), pp. 60-61.

[14] Le Drame Chrétien au Moyen Age (Paris, 1878).

[15] P. 31.

[16] Origines catholiques du théâtre moderne (Paris, 1904).

[17] E. Catherine Dunn, "Voice Structure in the Liturgical Drama: Sepet Reconsidered," Medieval English Drama, ed. Jerome Taylor and Alan H. Nelson (Chicago, 1972), p. 63.

[18] Histoire du théâtre en France: les Mystères (Paris, 1880), I, 21. See Léon Gautier, Histoire de la poésie liturgique au moyen âge: les tropes (Paris, 1886).

[19] Geschichte des neueren Dramas (Halle, 1893), I, 48.

[20] London, 1903.

[21] O. B. Hardison, Jr., Christian Rite and Christian Drama in the Middle Ages (Baltimore, 1965), p. 5.

[22] London, 1903.

[23] Cambridge, MA., 1924.

[24] London, 1933.

[25] New York, 1930.

[26] History of English Poetry from the 11th to the 17th Century (London, 1882). There were earlier editions in 1778 and 1781.

[27] The Life of Geoffrey Chaucer, the Early English Poet (London, 1803), I, 78-79.

[28] (The Hague, 1955), p. 116.

[29] Milano, 1938. For Voltaire's remark, see his Essai sur les moeurs et l'ésprit des nations, II, 377 in OEuvres Complètes (Paris, 1785).

[30] (Oxford, 1954), p. 23.

[31] London, 1955.

[32] "Literary Forms and the New Theory of the Origin of the Species," Modern Philology, IV (1906-7, 577-595.

[33] Toronto, 1958.

[34] "The Liturgical Drama and Its Tradition: A Review of Scholarship 1965-1975," Research Opportunities in Renaissance Drama, 18 (1975), 81-102; 19 (1976), 109-136.

[35] Flanigan, p. 136.

In an admirable article published after this book left its author's hands, David A. Bjork persuasively argues that the texts of the VS ought to be studied according to their geographical origin rather than chronologically. He concludes that the initial usage of the Quem Quaeritis speech cannot be determined nor can its prehistory before its use by Ethelwold. "On the Dissemination of Quem quaeritis and the Visitatio sepulchri and the Chronology of Their Early Sources," Comparative Drama, 14, 1 (1980), 46-69.

SELECTED BIBLIOGRAPHY

Primary Sources

Ademar de Chabannes, "Commemoratio Abbatum Lemovicensium," Chroniques de Saint-Martial de Limoges, ed. H. Duplès-Agier. Paris, 1874.

AElfricus. "Excerpta ex institutionibus monasticis AEthelwoldi Episcopi Wintoniensis...," Compotus Rolls of the Obedientiaries of St. Swithun's Priory, ed. G.W. Kitchen. London, 1892.

AEthelwoldus. "Edgar's Establishment of the Monasteries," Leechdoms, Wortcunning, and Starcraft in Early England, ed. Oswald Cockayne. Rerum Britannicarum Medii Aevi Scriptores, No. 35 (London, 1886), I, 441-442.

---. Regularis Concordia, ed. Thomas Symons. Nelson's Medieval Classics. London, 1953.

---. The Rule of St. Benedict in Die Angelsächsischen Prosabearbeitungen der Benedictinerregel, ed. Arnold Schörer. Kassell, 1888.

Anglo-Saxon Chronicle, ed. Dorothy Whitelock et al. New Brunswick, N.J., 1961.

"Annales Anglosaxonici breves (925-1202)," Ungedruckte Anglo-Normannische Geschichtquellen, ed. Felix Liebermann. Strasbourg, 1879.

"Les Annales Blandensis," Les Annales de Saint-Pierre de Gand et de Saint-Amand, ed. Philip Grierson (Bruxelles, 1937), pp. 1-73.

"Annales Corbiensis," Monumenta Germaniae Historica Scriptorum (Leipzig, 1826-1934), I, 1-18.

"Annales de Wintonia," Annales Monastici, ed. H.R. Luard. Rerum Britannicarum Medii Aevi Scriptores, No. 36 (London, 1865), II, 11ff.

"Annales Sancti Bavonis Gandensis," Recueil des Chroniques de Flandre, ed. J.-J. de Smet (Bruxelles, 1837), I, 439-451.

The Benedictional of Archbishop Robert, ed. H.A. Wilson. Publications of the Henry Bradshaw Society. London, 1903.

The Benedictional of Saint-AEthelwold, Bishop of Winchester, 963-984, ed. George F. Warner and H.A. Wilson. Oxford, 1910.

The Black Book of Winchester, ed. W.H.B. Bird. Winchester, 1925.

The Blicking Homilies of the Tenth Century, ed. R. Morris. Early English Text Society, O.S. 58. London, 1880.

The Bosworth Psalter, ed. F.A. Gasquet and E. Bishop. London, 1908.

The Cartulary of Worcester Cathedral Priory, ed. R.R. Darlington. London, 1968.

Chartulary of Winchester Cathedral, ed. A.W. Goodman. Winchester, 1927.

Chronicon Abbatiae Rameseiensis, a Saec. X. usque ad An. circiter 1200, ed. W. Dunn Macray. Rerum Britannicarum Medii Aevi Scriptores, No. 83. London, 1886.

Chronicon Monasterii de Abingdon, ed. Joseph Stevenson. 2 vols. Rerum Britannicarum Medii Aevi Scriptores, No. 2. London, 1888.

"Chronicon Sancti Bavonis Scriptum sub Finem Seculi XV ab auctore anonymo," Recueil des Chroniques de Flandre, ed. J.-J. de Smet (Bruxelles, 1837), I, 455-588.

"Consuetudines insignis monasterii Sancti Vitoni Verdunensis," De Antiquis
    Ecclesiae Ritibus, ed. Edmund Martene. Vol. IV. Antwerp, 1736.

"Episcopus," Die Gesetze der Angelsachsen, ed. Felix Liebermann (Halle,
    1903), I, 477-479.

Fabii Ethelwerdi Chronicorum libri quattuor, trans. J. A. Giles. London, 1848.

"Gerefa," ed. Felix Liebermann, Anglia, IX (1886), 251-266.

"Gesta Episcorum Virdunensium auctoribus Bertario et anonymo monachis St.
    Vitoni," Patrologia Latina, ed. J.-P. Migne (Paris, 1844-1904),
    CXXXII, 502-528.

The Historians of the Church of York and Its Archbishops, ed. James Raine.
    3 vols. Rerum Britannicarum Medii Aevi Scriptores, No. 71. London,
    1879.

Jocelin of Brakelond. Monastic and Social Life in the Twelfth Century..., trans.
    T. E. Tomlins. London, 1884.

Liber Eliensis, ed. E. O. Blake. Publications of the Royal Historical Society,
    Camden 3rd ser., No. 92. London, 1962.

Liber Monasterii de Hyda, ed. Edward Edwards. Rerum Britannicarum Medii
    Aevi, No. 45. London, 1866.

Liber Traditionum S. Petri Blandiensis, ed. Arnold Fayen. Ghent, 1906.

Liber Vitae: Register and Martyrology of New Minster and Hyde Abbey, Win-
    chester, ed. Walter de Gray Birch. London, 1892.

"Liber Winton," Domesday Book, seu Libri Censualis, Willelmi Primi Regis
    Angliae, Addimento ex. Codic. Antiquiss. Great Britain Public Records
    Commission, IV (1816), 529-562.

Memorials of St. Dunstan, ed. William Stubbs. Rerum Britannicarum Medii
    Aevi Scriptores, No. 63. London, 1874.

Missal of St. Augustine's Abbey, Canterbury, ed. M. Rule. Cambridge, 1896.

The Monastic Breviary of Hyde Abbey, Winchester, ed. J. B. L. Tolhurst. 6
    vols. Publications of the Henry Bradshaw Society. London, 1932.

"Nomina Monachorum vivorum et mortuorum Ecclesie Xpi. Cant. a tempore
    exilii 1207 ad annum 1533," ed. Robert Causton. Great Britain Histori-
    cal Manuscrpts Commission, 9th Report, Pt. 1 (London, 1883), 127ff.

The Ordinale and Customary of the Benedictine Nuns of Barking Abbey, ed.
    J. B. L. Tolhurst. 2 vols. Publications of the Henry Bradshaw Society,
    No. 56. London, 1928.

Osbernus. "Vita Sancti Elphegi... auctore Osberno," Patrologia Latina, ed.
    J.-P. Migne (Paris, 1844-1904), CXLIX, 371-386.

"Rectitudines sive Singularum Personarum," Ancient Laws and Institutes of
    England, ed. Benjamin Thorpe. London, 1840.

Registrum Hamonis Hethe Diocesis Roffensis A. D. 1319-1353, ed. Charles
    Johnson. 2 vols. Canterbury and York Series, No. 41. Oxford, 1948.

Rituale Ecclesiae Dunelmensis, ed. Joseph Stevenson. Publications of the
    Surtees Society, No. 10. London, 1840.

The Rule of St. Benedict, ed. and trans. Hunter Blair. Fort Augustus, Scot.,
    1948.

The Rule of St. Benedict, ed. Justin McCann. London, 1951.

The Rule of St. Benet: Latin and Anglo-Saxon, ed. H. Logeman. Early English
  Text Society, O. S. 99. London, 1888.
St. Dunstan's Classbook from Glastonbury, intro. R. W. Hunt. Umbrae Codicum
  Occidentalium, No. 4. Amsterdam, 1961.
Scriptorum Brunsuicensia Illustrantium, ed. G. W. Leibnitz. 3 vols. Hanover,
  1711.
Three Middle English Versions of the Rule of St. Benet, ed. Ernest O. Kock.
  Early English Text Society, O. S. 120. London, 1902.
"Vita Odonis," Anglia Sacra, ed. Thomas Wharton. 2 vols. London, 1691.
"Vita Odonis," Historians of the Church of York and Its Archbishops, ed.
  James Raine (London, 1879), I, 400-410.
"Vita S. AEthelwoldi episcopi Wintoniensis auctore AElfrico," Chronicon
  Monasterii de Abingdon, ed. Joseph Stevenson (London, 1858), II, 253-
  256.
"Vita Sancti AEthelwoldi auctore Wulstano," Patrologia Latina, ed. J.-P.
  Migne (Paris, 1844-1904), CXXXVIII, 79-114.
"Vita Sancti Dunstani auctore Adelardo," Memorials of St. Dunstan, ed William
  Stubbs (London, 1874), p. 53ff.
"Vita Sancti Dunstani auctore B." Memorials of St. Dunstan, ed. William
  Stubbs (London, 1874), p. 3ff.
"Vita Sancti Dunstani auctore Eadmero," Memorials of St. Dunstan, ed. William
  Stubbs (London, 1874), p. 162ff.
"Vita Sancti Dunstani auctore Osberno," Memorials of St. Dunstan, ed. William
  Stubbs (London, 1874), p. 69ff.
"Vita Sancti Dunstani auctore Willelmi Malmesburiensis," Memorials of St.
  Dunstan, ed. William Stubbs (London, 1874), p. 250ff.
"Vita Sancti Elphegi... auctore Osberno," Patrologia Latina, ed. J.-P. Migne
  (Paris, 1844-1904), CXLIX, 371-386.
"Vita Sancti Oswaldi auctore anonymo," Historians of the Church of York and
  Its Archbishops, ed. James Raine (London, 1879), I, 399-475.
"Vita Sancti Oswaldi auctore Eadmero," Historians of the Church of York and
  Its Archbishops, ed. James Raine (London, 1879), II, 1ff.
"De Wergildis Singularum Personarum cum Anglis," Ancient Laws and Institutes,
  ed. Benjamin Thorpe. London, 1840.
Willelmi Malmesburiensis. "De Gestis Pontificum Anglorum," Patrologia Latina,
  J.-P. Migne (Paris, 1844-1904), CLXXIX, 1441-1680.
---.   "Liber de Antiquitate Glastoniensis Ecclesiae," Patrologia Latina, ed.
  J.-P. Migne (Paris, 1844-1904), CLXXIX, 1681-1734.
The Winchester Troper from Manuscripts of the Xth and XIth Centuries, ed.
  W. H. Frere. London, 1894.
Wulstanus. The Benedictine Office: An Old English Text, ed. James M. Ure.
  Edinburgh University Publications in Language and Literature, No. 11.
  Edinburgh, 1957.

Books

Anderson, M.D. Drama and Imagery in English Medieval Churches. Cambridge, 1963.

Andrews, Charles M. The Old English Manor: A Study in English Economical History. Baltimore, 1892.

Anglo-Saxon England 1, ed. Peter Clemoes et al. Cambridge, 1972.

Anglo-Saxon England 3, ed. Peter Clemoes et al. Cambridge, 1974.

The Antiquities of Winchester. Winchester, 1850(?).

Apel, Willi. Gregorian Chant. Bloomington, Ind., 1958.

---. The Notation of Polyphonic Music 900-1600, 5th ed. Cambridge, MA., 1953.

Aspects of Medieval and Renaissance Music: A Birthday Offering to Gustave Reese, ed. Jan La Rue. New York, 1966.

Axton, Richard. European Drama of the Early Middle Ages. London, 1974.

Barlow, Frank. The English Church, 1000-1066. London, 1963.

Barraclough, Geoffrey. The Crucible of Europe: The 9th and 10th Centuries in European History. Berkeley, 1976.

Baxter, J.H. and Charles Johnson. Medieval Latin Word-List from British and Irish Sources. Oxford, 1947.

Bennett, J.S. Life on the English Manor: A Study of Peasant Conditions 1150-1400. Cambridge, 1938.

Berger, Blandine Dominique. Le Drame liturgique de Pâques en Xe au XIIIe Siècles: Liturgie et Théâtre. Paris, 1976.

Biddle, Martin. The Old Minster: Excavations near Winchester Cathedral 1961-1969. Winchester, 1970.

---. ed. Winchester in the Early Middle Ages: An Edition and Discussion of the Winton Domesday. Winchester Studies, No. 1. Oxford, 1976.

Birch, Walter de Gray. Cartularium Saxonici, 3 vols. London, 1885-93.

---. Fasti Monastici Aevi Saxonici: or, An Alphabetical List of the Heads of the Religious Houses in England Prior to the Norman Conquest. London, 1872.

Blair, Peter Hunter. An Introduction to Anglo-Saxon England. Cambridge, 1962.

Boileau-Despreau, Nicolas. L'Art Poètique, ed. D. Nicholas Smith. Cambridge, 1898.

Britton, John. The History and Antiquities of the See and Cathedral Church of Winchester.... London, 1817.

Brockett, Oscar, G. History of the Theatre. Boston, 1968.

Brooke, Christopher. From Alfred to Henry III, 871-1271. London, 1961.

Brooks, Neil C. The Sepulchre of Christ in Art and Liturgy: with Special Reference to the Liturgic Drama. University of Illinois Studies in Language and Literature, VII, 2 (May 1921), 1-110.

Brown, G. Baldwin. The Arts in Early England, 4 vols. London, 1926.

Browne, Willis. An History of the Mitred Parliamentary Abbies, and Conventual Churches, 2 vols. London, 1719.

Bruce-Mitford, R.L.S. The Sutton Hoo Ship Burial. London, 1968

Butler, Cuthbert. Benedictine Monachism: Studies in Benedictine Life and Rule. Cambridge, 1924.

duCange, Domino. Glossarium Mediae et Infimae Latinitatis, 10 vols. Paris, 1938.

Cargill, Oscar. Drama and Liturgy. New York, 1930.

Cassan, Stephen H. The Lives of the Bishops of Winchester, from Birinus, the First Bishop of the West Saxons, to the Present Time, 2 vols. London, 1827.

Chailley, Jacques. L'Ecole Musicale de Saint-Martial de Limoges jusqu'à la Fin du XIe Siècle. Paris, 1960.

Chambers, Edmund K. The Mediaeval Stage, 2 vols. London, 1903.

---. A Sheaf of Studies. London, 1942.

Chirat, Henri. Dictionnaire Latin-Français des Auteurs Chrétiens. Strasbourg, 1954.

Churchill, Winston S. The Birth of Britain. History of the English-Speaking Peoples, Vol. I. New York, 1958.

Clapham, A.W. English Romanesque Architecture before the Conquest. Oxford, 1930.

Coffman, George R. A New Theory concerning the Origin of the Miracle Play. Menasha, Wis., 1914.

Cohen, Gustave. Le Théâtre français en Belgique au Moyen Age. Bruxelles, 1953.

Collins, Fletcher, Jr. Medieval Church Music-Drama: A Repertory of Complete Plays. Charlottesville, VA., 1976.

---. The Production of Medieval Church Music-Drama. Charlottesville, VA., 1972.

Constable, Giles. Monastic Tithes from Their Origins to the Twelfth Century. Cambridge, 1964.

Corbin, Solange. La Déposition liturgique du Christ au vendredi saint: sa place dans l'histoire des rites et du théâtre religieux. Paris, 1960.

Cottas, Vénétia. Le Théâtre à Byzance. Paris, 1931.

Coussemaker, Edouard de. Drames liturgiques du Moyen Age. Rennes, 1860.

Craig, Hardin. English Religious Drama of the Middle Ages. London, 1955.

Creizenach, Wilhelm. Geschichte des neuren Dramas, 4 vols. Halle, 1893.

Cutts, Edward L. Parish Priests and Their People in the Middle Ages in England. London, 1898.

Dauphin, H. Le bienheureux Richard, Abbé de Saint-Vanne de Verdun, 1046. Louvain, 1946.

Deanesly, Margaret. The Pre-Conquest Church in England. London, 1963.

---. Sidelights on the Anglo-Saxon Church. London, 1962.

De Boor, Helmut. Die Textgeschichte der Lateinischen Osterfeiern. Tübingen, 1967.

Dickinson, J.C. Monastic Life in Medieval England. London, 1961.

Diller, Hans-Jürgen. Redeformen des englischen Misterienspiels. München, 1973.

Dodwell, C.R., ed. The English Church and the Continent. London, 1959.

Dolan, Diane. Le Drame liturgique de Pâques en Normandie et en Angleterre au Moyen Age. Paris, 1975.

Donovan, Richard B. The Liturgical Drama in Medieval Spain. Toronto, 1958.

Duckett, Eleanor S. Death and Life in the Tenth Century. Ann Arbor, 1960.

———. Saint Dunstan of Canterbury. London, 1955.

Dugdale, William. Monasticon Anglicanum, 6 vols. London, 1846.

Dunn, E. Catherine et al., eds. The Medieval Drama and Its Claudelian Revival. Washington, D.C., 1970.

Edwards, Francis. Ritual and Drama: The Mediaeval Theatre. Guildford, 1976.

Edwards, Kathleen. The English Secular Cathedrals in the Middle Ages. Manchester, 1967.

Else, Gerald F. The Origin and Early Form of Greek Tragedy. Martin Classical Lectures, No. 20. Cambridge, MA., 1965.

Evans, Joan. Monastic Life at Cluny, 910-1157. New York, 1968.

Evans, Paul. The Early Trope Repertory of St. Martial of Limoges. Princeton, 1970.

Feasey, H.J. Ancient English Holy Week Ceremonial. London, 1897.

Fellows, George E. The Anglo-Saxon Towns and Their Polity. Bern, 1890.

Fichte, Jörg O. Expository Voices in Medieval Drama: Essays on the Mode and Function of Dramatic Exposition. Nürnberg, 1975.

Flemming, Willi. Die Gestaltung der liturgischen Osterfeier in Deutschland. Mainz, 1971.

Fontenelle, Bernard le Bovier de. OEuvres, 8 vols. Paris, 1742.

Frank, Grace. The Medieval French Drama. Oxford, 1954.

Furley, J.S. The Ancient Usages of the City of Winchester. Oxford, 1927.

Gautier, Léon. Histoire de la poésie liturgique au moyen âge: les tropes. Paris, 1886.

Gervais, Abbé de la Rue. Essais historiques sur les bardes, les jongleurs, et les trouvières normands et anglo-normands. Caen, 1834.

Gilbert, H.M. and G.W. Godwin. Bibliotheca Hantoniensis: A List of Books Relating to Hampshire.... Southampton, 1891.

Godfrey, John. The Church in Anglo-Saxon England. Cambridge, 1962.

Godwin, William. The Life of Geoffrey Chaucer, the Early English Poet. 2 vols. London, 1803.

Graham, Rose. English Ecclesiastical Studies. London, 1929.

Grégoire de Nazianze. La Passion du Christ, ed. and trans. André Tuilier. Sources Chrétiennes, No. 49. Paris, 1969.

Hardison, O.B., Jr. Christian Rite and Christian Drama in the Middle Ages. Baltimore, 1965.

Harmer, F.E., ed. Select English Historical Documents of the 9th and 10th Centuries. London, 1914.

Hastings, Charles. The Theatre: Its Development in France and England. Trans. Frances A. Welby. London, 1901.

Heitz, Carol. Recherches sur les rapports entre architecture et liturgie à l'époque carolingienne. Paris, 1963.

Heywood, Samuel. A Dissertation upon the Distinctions in Society and Ranks of the People under the Anglo-Saxon Governments. London, 1818.

Hildburgh, W. L. English Alabaster Carvings as Records of the Medieval Religious Drama. Oxford, 1949.

Hill, Geoffry. English Dioceses: A History of Their Limits from Earliest Times to the Present Day. London, 1900.

Hodgkin, Robert H. A History of the Anglo-Saxons, 2 vols. London, 1939.

Holland, L. B. Traffic Ways about France in the Dark Ages, 500-1150. Allentown, PA., 1919.

Holschneider, Andreas. Die Organa von Winchester. Hildesheim, 1968.

Hone, Nathaniel J. The Manor and Manorial Records, 3rd ed. London, 1925.

Hoppin, Richard H. Medieval Music. New York, 1978.

Hughes, H. D. A History of Durham Cathedral Library. Durham, 1925.

Hunningher, Benjamin. The Origin of the Theatre. The Hague, 1955.

Inman, A. H. Domesday and Feudal Statistics. London, 1900.

James, M. R. The Ancient Libraries of Canterbury and Dover. Cambridge, 1903.

---. On the Abbey of S. Edmund at Bury. Cambridge, 1895.

John, Eric. Land Tenure in Early England. Leicester, 1960.

---. Orbis Britanniae and Other Studies. Leicester, 1966.

---. ed. The Popes. New York, 1964.

Jones, Cheslyn et al., eds. The Study of Liturgy. New York, 1978.

Jones, Leslie W. and C. R. Morey. The Miniatures of the Manuscripts of Terence prior to the 13th Century, 2 vols. Princeton, 1931-32.

Karhl, Stanley J. Traditions of Medieval English Drama. London, 1974.

Kendrick, T. D. Late Saxon and Viking Art. London, 1949.

Kirby, D. P. The Making of Early England. New York, 1967.

Knowles, David. Christian Monasticism. New York, 1969.

---. The Evolution of Medieval Thought. New York, 1962.

---. The Monastic Order in England, 2nd ed. London, 1963.

Konigson, Elie. L'Espace Théâtral Médiéval. Paris, 1975.

Kretzmann, Paul E. The Liturgical Element in the Earliest Forms of the Medieval Drama with Special Reference to the English and German Plays. University of Minnesota Studies in Language and Literature, No. 4. Minneapolis, 1916.

Lange, C. Die lateinischen Osterfeiern. München, 1887.

Lasteyrie, Charles de. L'Abbaye de Saint-Martial de Limoges. Paris, 1901.

Leach, Arthur F. Educational Charters and Documents, 598 to 1909. Cambridge, 1911.

Lindsay, Jack. Byzantium into Europe. London, 1952.

Lipphardt, Walther. Lateinische Osterfeiern und Osterspiele. Berlin, 1975.

Littlehales, H. Romsey Abbey, or, A History of the Benedictine Nunnery Founded in the 10th Century in Hampshire. Romsey, 1886.

Lopez, Robert S. The Tenth Century: How Dark the Dark Ages? New York, 1959.

Loyn, H. R. Anglo-Saxon England and the Norman Conquest. London, 1962.

---. The Vikings in Britain. New York, 1977.

Madox, Thomas. Firma Burgi: or, an Historical Essay concerning the Cities, Towns, and Boroughs of England. London, 1726.

Magnin, Charles. Les Origines du théâtre moderne. Paris, 1838.

Maitland, F. W. Domesday Book and Beyond. Cambridge, 1897.

Maître, Léon. Les Ecoles épiscopales et monastiques en occident avant les universités, 768-1180. Paris, 1924.

Mâle, Emile. L'Art religieux du XIIIe siècle en France, 3rd ed. Paris, 1928.

Martene, Edmund. De Antiquis Ecclesiae Ritibus, 4 vols. Antwerp, 1736.

Mediaevalia Litteraria: Festschrift für Helmut De Boor zum 80 Geburtstag, ed. Ursula Henning and Herbert Kolb. München, 1971.

Medieval English Drama: Essays Critical and Contextual, ed. Jerome Taylor and Alan H. Nelson. Chicago, 1972.

Meril, Edelstand Pontas du. Les Origines latines du théâtre moderne. Paris, 1897.

Michael, Wolfgang F. Das deutsche Drama des Mittelalters. Berlin, 1971.

Miller, Edward. The Abbey and Bishopric of Ely. Cambridge, 1966.

Moorman, J. R. H. A History of the Church in England, 2nd ed. London, 1967.

Nagler, A. M. The Medieval Religious Stage. New Haven, 1976.

New Paleographical Society. Facsimilies of Ancient Manuscripts, ed. E. M. Tomlin et al., 2 vols. London, 1903-12.

Nicoll, Allardyce. The Development of the Theatre. New York, 1958.

---. Masks, Mimes, and Miracles: Studies in the Popular Theatre. New York, 1963.

Pächt, Otto. The Rise of Pictorial Narrative in 12th-Century England. Oxford, 1962.

Page, William, ed. A History of Hampshire and the Isle of Wight, 5 vols. The Victoria History of the Counties of England. Westminster, 1900-12.

Parsons, David, ed. Tenth-Century Studies: Essays in Commemoration of the Millennium of the Council of Winchester and Regularis Concordia. London, 1975.

Parfaict, François et Charles. Histoire du théâtre françois depuis son origine jusqu'à présent, 15 vols. Paris, 1734-49.

Perry, G. G. A History of the English Church, 5th ed. London, 1890.

Petit de Julleville, Louis. Histoire du théâtre en France: les Mystères. Paris, 1880.

Petrie, Henry and John Sharpe, eds. Monumenta Historica Britannica, 2 vols. Great Britain Public Records Commission. London, 1848.

Pierik, Marie. The Spirit of Gregorian Chant. Boston, 1939.

Pierquin, Hubert. Recueil général des chartes Anglo-Saxonnes. Paris, 1912.

Planchart, Alejandro Enrique. The Repertory of Tropes at Winchester, 2 vols. Princeton, 1977.

Powicke, F. M. Handbook of British Chronology, 2nd ed. London, 1961.

Price, Mary R. Bede and Dunstan. London, 1968.

Report of the 10th Congress, Ljubljana 1967, ed. Dragotin Cvetko. Kassel, 1970.

Rice, D. Talbot. English Art, 871-1100. The Oxford History of Art, ed. T. S. R. Boase. Oxford, 1952.

Riché, Pierre. Daily Life in the World of Charlemagne. Trans. Jo Ann McNamara. Philadelphia, 1978.

Robertson, A. J., ed. Anglo-Saxon Charters. Cambridge, 1939.

---. The Laws of the Kings of England from Edmund to Henry I. London, 1925.

Robinson, J. A. St. Oswald and the Church of Worcester. London, 1919.

---. The Times of St. Dunstan. London, 1922.

Rock, Daniel. The Church of Our Fathers as Seen in St. Osmund's Rite for the Cathedral of Salisbury, ed. G. W. Hart and W. H. Frere. 4 vols. London, 1905.

Roeder, Anke. Die Gebärde im Drama des Mittelalters. München, 1974.

Rolfe, C. C. The Ancient Use of Liturgical Colors. Oxford, 1879.

Roston, Murray. Biblical Drama in England from the Middle Ages to the Present Day. London, 1968.

Sawyer, P. H. Anglo-Saxon Charters: An Annotated List and Bibliography. London, 1968.

Schlegel, A. W. Lectures on Dramatic Art and Literature, trans. John Black. London, 1883.

Schroer, Arnold. Die angelsächsischen Prosabearbeitungen der Benedictiner-regel. Kassel, 1888.

Scott, Gilbert. Essay on the History of English Church Architecture. London, 1881.

Selden, Samuel. Man in His Theatre. Chapel Hill, N. C., 1957.

Sepet, Marius. Le Drame Chrétien au Moyen Age. Paris, 1878.

---. Origines catholiques du théâtre moderne. Paris, 1904.

---. Les Prophètes du Christ. Paris, 1867.

Smith, L. M. The Early History of Cluny. London, 1920.

Spencer, Herbert. The Principles of Psychology, 2 vols. New York, 1910.

Stael-Holstein, Germaine de. De l'Allemagne, 3rd ed. Paris, 1815.

Stemmler, Theo. Liturgische Feiern und Geistliche Spiele. Tübingen, 1970.

Stenton, Frank M. Anglo-Saxon England, 2nd ed. Oxford, 1947.

Stephens, William and W. W. Capes. The Bishops of Winchester, 2 vols. Winchester, 1907.

Stevens, John. The History of the Antient Abbeys, Monasteries, Hospitals, Cathedrals and Collegiate Churches..., 2 vols. London, 1722.

Sticca, Sandro. The Latin Passion Play: Its Origins and Development. Albany, 1970.

---. ed. The Medieval Drama. Albany, 1972.

Stuart, Donald C. Stage Decoration in France in the Middle Ages. Columbia University Studies in Romance Philogogy and Literature. New York, 1910.

Studies in the Arts: Proceedings of the St. Peter's College Literary Society, ed. Francis Warner, Oxford, 1968.

Tait, J. The Medieval English Borough. Manchester, 1936.

Tanner, Thomas. Notitia Monastica: or, An Account of All the Abbies, Priories, and Houses of Friars formerly in England and Wales.... Cambridge, 1787.

Thorpe, Benjamin, ed. Ancient Laws and Institutes of England, 2 vols. London, 1840.

---. Diplomatarium Anglicum Aevi Saxonici. London, 1865.

Tunison, Joseph S. Dramatic Traditions of the Dark Ages. Chicago, 1907.

Turner, Barbara C. The Churches of Medieval Winchester. Winchester, 1957.

Tydeman, William. The Theatre in the Middle Ages: Western European Stage Conditions, c. 800-1576. Cambridge, 1978.

Ussher, James. The Whole Works of James Ussher. Dublin, 1847-64.

Valous, Guy de. Monachisme clunisien des origines au XVe siècle. 2 vols. Paris, 1935.

Vito, Maria Sofia de. L'Origine de Dramma Liturgico. Milano, 1938.

Voltaire, François Marie Arouet de. Essai sur les moeurs et l'esprit des nations in OEuvres Complètes, 70 vols. Paris, 1785.

Warton, Thomas. A Description of the City, College, and Cathedral of Winchester. London, 1760.

---. The History and Antiquities of Winchester..., 2 vols. Winchester, 1773.

---. A History of English Poetry from the 11th to the 17th Century. London, 1778.

Wellesz, Egon. Eastern Elements in Western Chant: Studies in the Early History of Ecclesiastical Music. Copenhagen, 1946.

Werner, Wilfried. Studien zu den Passions- und Osterspielen des deutschen Mittelalters in ihren Uebergang vom Latein zur Volkssprache. Berlin, 1963.

Wharton, Henry. Anglia Sacra, sive, Collectio Historiarum...Archiepiscopis et Episcopis Angliae, 2 vols. London, 1691.

Whitelock, Dorothy. The Beginnings of English Society. Harmondsworth, 1962.

---. ed. English Historical Documents, c. 500-1042. London, 1968.

Wickham, Glynne. Early English Stages, 2 vols. London, 1963.

---. The Medieval Theatre. London, 1974.

---. Shakespeare's Dramatic Heritage. London, 1969.

Williams, Arnold. The Drama of Medieval England. E. Lansing, Mich., 1961.

Williamson, J. Glastonbury Abbey: Its History and Ruins. Wells, 1862.

Wilson, R. M. The Lost Literature of Medieval England, 2nd ed. London, 1970.

Winckelmann, Johanne J. History of Ancient Art, trans. G. Henry Lodge. 2 vols. Boston, 1872.

Woodland, Walter. The Story of Winchester. London, 1932.

Workman, Herbert B. The Evolution of the Monastic Ideal. London, 1913.

Wormald, Francis. English Drawings of the 10th and 11th Centuries. London, 1952.

Wright, Edith A. The Dissemination of the Liturgical Drama in France. Bryn Mawr, PA., 1936.

Young, Karl. The Drama of the Medieval Church, 2 vols. London, 1933.

Articles

Albers, Bruno. "Les 'Consuetudines Sigeberti Abbatis'," Revue Bénédictine, XX (1903), 420-433.

Allen, Philip S. "The Mediaeval Mimus, II," Modern Philology, VIII (1910-11), 17-60.

Apel, Willi. "Early History of the Organ," Speculum, XXIII (1948), 191-216.

Atkins, Ivor. "The Church of Worcester from the 8th to the 12th Century," The Antiquaries Journal, XVII (1937), 371-391.

Ayer, Joseph C. "Church Councils of the Anglo-Saxons," American Society of Church History Papers, 2nd. ser., VII (1937), 91-107.

Bateson, Mary. "Rules for Monks and Secular Canons after the Revival under King Edgar," English Historical Review, IX (1894), 690-708.

Beddie, James S. "The Ancient Classics in Mediaeval Libraries," Speculum, V (1930), 3-20.

Berlière, Usmer. "Coutumiers monastiques," Revue Bénédictine, XXIX (1912), 355-367.

Biddle, Martin. "Excavations at Winchester, 1963," The Antiquaries Journal, XLIV (1964), 188-219.

---. "Excavations at Winchester, 1964," The Antiquaries Journal, XVL (1965), 230-264.

---. "Excavations at Winchester, 1965," The Antiquaries Journal, XLVI (1966), 308-332.

---. "Winchester," Archaeological Journal, CXXIII (1966), 182-183.

---. Gabrielle Lambrick, and J.N.L. Myres. "The Early History of Abingdon, Berks., and Its Abbey," Mediaeval Archaeology, XII (1968), 26-69.

Bittermann, H.B. "The Organ in the Early Middle Ages," Speculum, IV (1929), 390-410.

Bogdanos, Theodore. "Liturgical Drama in Byzantine Literature," Comparative Drama, 10 (1976-77), 200-215.

Bonnell, J.K. "The Easter Sepulchrum in Its Relation to the Architecture of the High Altar," PMLA, XXXI (1916), 664-711.

Bréhier, Louis. "Les Colonies d'Orientaux en Occident," Byzantinische Zeitschrift, XII (1903), 1-39.

Brooks, Neil C. "Osterfeiern aus Bamberger und Wolfenbüttler Handschriften," Zeitschrift für Deutsches Altertum und Deutsche Litteratur, LV (1914), 52-61.

Campbell, A. "The End of the Kingdom of Northumbria," English Historical Review, LVII (1942), 91-97.

Chambers, E.K. "The Study of English Literature," A Sheaf of Studies (London, 1942).

Coffman, G.R. "A New Approach to Medieval Latin Drama," Modern Philology, XXII (1924-25), 239-271.

Crocker, Richard. "The Troping Hypothesis," Musical Quarterly, 52 (1966), 183-203.

Cunliffe, Barry. "Saxon Culture Sequence at Portchester Castle," The Antiquaries Journal, L (1970), 67-85.

Dauphin, H. "Le Renouveau monastique en Angleterre au Xe siècle et ses rapports avec la reforme de saint Gérard de Brogne," Revue Bénédictine, LXX (1960), 177-196.

Deanesly, Margaret. "Early English and Gallic Minsters," Transactions of the Royal Historical Society, 4th ser., XXIII (1941), 25-69.

Dunn, E. Catherine. "Popular Devotion in the Vernacular Drama of Medieval England," Medievalia et Humanistica, N.S. 4 (1973), 55-68.

Else, Gerald F. "The Origin of ΤΡΑΓΩΙΔΙΑ," Hermes: Zeitschrift für Klassische Philologie, LXXXV (1957), 17-46.

Evans, Paul. "Some Reflections on the Origin of the Trope," Journal of the American Musicological Society, 14 (1961), 119-130.

Fisher, D.J.V. "The Anti-Monastic Reaction in the Reign of Edward the Martyr," Cambridge Historical Journal, X (1952), 254-270.

---. "The Early Biographers of St. Ethelwold," English Historical Review, LXVII (1952), 38-91.

Flanigan, C. Clifford. "The Liturgical Context of the Quem Quaeritis Trope," Comparative Drama, 8 (1974), 45-62.

---. "The Liturgical Drama and Its Tradition: A Review of Scholarship 1965-1975," Research Opportunities in Renaissance Drama, 18 (1975), 81-102; 19 (1976), 109-136.

---. "The Roman Rite and the Origins of the Liturgical Drama," University of Toronto Quarterly, 43 (1974), 263-284.

Gage, John. "A Description of a Benedictional, or Pontifical, called 'Benedictionarius Roberti Archiepiscopi', an illuminated Manuscript of the tenth century, in the Public Library at Rouen...," Archaeologia, XXIV (1832), 118-136.

---. "A Dissertation on St. AEthelwold's Benedictional, an Illuminated Manuscript of the Tenth Century," Archaeologia, XXIV (1832), 1-117.

Gambraith, Vivian H. "Royal Charters to Winchester," English Historical Review, XXV (1920), 382-400.

Gamer, Helena M. "Mimes, Musicians, and the Origin of the Mediaeval Religious Play," Deutsche Beiträge zur Geistigen Ueberlieferung, V (1965), 9-28.

Goethe, J.W. von. "Winckelmann und sein Jahrhundert," Schriften zur Kunst in Gedenkausgabe der Werke, Briefe und Gespräche (Zürich, 1954), XIII, 407-450.

Gougaud, L. "Les Relations de l'abbaye de Fleury-sur-Loire avec Bretagne armoricaine et les îles britanniques (Xe et XIe siècles)," Memoires Société Historique et Archéologique de Bretagne, IV (1923), 3-30.

Graham, Rose. "The Intellectual Influence of English Monasticism between the 10th and the 12th Centuries," Transactions of the Royal Historical Society, N.S. XVII (1903), 21-65.

---. "The Relation of Cluny to Some Other Movements of Monastic Reform," Journal of Theological Studies, XV (1914), 179-195.

Grattan-Flood, W.H. "The Irish Origin of the Easter Play," The Month, CXLI (1923), 349-353.

Grierson, Philip, "The Relation between England and Flanders before the Norman Conquest," Transactions of the Royal Historical Society, 4th ser., XXIII (1941), 71-112.

Handschin, Jacques. "Trope, Sequence, Conductus," Early Medieval Music up to 1300, ed. A. Hughes. New Oxford History of Music, Vol. 2. Oxford, 1954.

Husmann, Heinrich. "Sinn und Wesen der Tropen veranschaulicht an den Introitustropen des Weihnachtsfestes," Archiv für Musikwissenschaft, 16 (1959), 137-147.

Hyde, Walter W. "The 200th Anniversary of the Birth of Winckelmann," The Monist, XXVIII (1918), 76-122.

Irvine, J.T. "Account of the Discovery of Part of the Saxon Abbey Church of Peterborough," Journal of the British Archaeological Association, L (1894), 45-54.

Jodogne, Omer. "Recherches sur les débuts du théâtre religieux en France," Cahiers de civilisation médiévale, VIII (1965), 179-189.

John, Eric. "The Beginning the Benedictine Reform in England," Revue Bénédictine, LXXIII (1963), 73-88.

---. "The King and the Monks in the 10th Century Reformation," Bulletin of the John Rylands Library, XLI (1959), 64-87.

---. "St. Oswald and the 10th Century Reformation," Journal of Ecclesiastical History, IX (1958), 159-172.

---. "The Sources of the English Monastic Reformation," Revue Bénédictine, LXX (1960), 197-203.

John, Otto. "The History of the Ancient Arts among the Greeks," The Westminster Review, LXXXVII (1867), 36-50.

Keim, H.W. "AEthelwold und die Monchreform in England," Anglia, XLI (1917), 405-443.

Klapper, J. "Der Ursprung der Lateinischen Osterfeiern," Zeitschrift für deutsche Philologie, 50 (1923), 46-58.

Knowles, David. "The Cultural Influence of English Medieval Monasticism," Cambridge Historical Journal, VII (1941-43), 146-159.

---. "The Monastic Horarium, 970-1120," Downside Review, LI (1933), 501-522.

---. "Monastic Parish Organization," Downside Review, LI (1933), 501-522.

Lehmann, Paul. "The Benedictine Order and the Transmission of the Literature of Ancient Rome in the Middle Ages," Erforschung des Mittelalters, III (1960), 173-183.

Liegey, Gabriel M. "Faith and the Origin of Liturgical Art," Thought, XXII (1947), 126-138.

Mancini, Valentino. "Public et espace scénique dans le théâtre du moyen âge," Revue d'histoire du théâtre, 17 (1965), 387-403.

Manly, John M. "Literary Forms and the New Theory of the Origin of the Species," Modern Philology, IV (1906-7), 577-595.

"Les Manuscrits de Saint-Marital de Limoges," Bulletin de la Société Archéologique et Historique du Limousin, XLIII (1895), 1-60.

Mathieu, Michel. "Distanciation et émotion dans le théâtre liturgique au moyen âge," Revue d'histoire du théâtre, 21 (1969), 95-117.

McGee, Timothy J. "The Liturgical Placements of the Quem Quaeritis Dialogue," Journal of the American Musicological Society, 29 (1976), 1-29.

Meyer, P. "Les Trois Maries," Romania, XXXIII (1904), 239-245.

Michael, Wolfgang. "Tradition and Originality in the Medieval Drama in Germany," The Medieval Drama, ed. Sandro Sticca (Albany, 1972), pp. 23-37.

Morin, D.G. "Le Catalogue des Manuscrits de l'Abbaye de Gorze au Xe siècle," Revue Bénédictine, XXII (1905), 1-14.

Muller, H. F. "Pre-history of the Medieval Drama: The Antecedents of the Tropes and the Conditions of Their Appearance," Zeitschrift für romanische Philologie, XLIV (1924-25), 544-575.

Odelman, Eva. "Comment a-t-on appelé les tropes? Observations sur les rubrique des tropes des Xe et XIe siècles," Cahiers de Civilisation Médiévale, 18 (1975), 15-36.

Ogilvy, J. D. A. "Mimi, Scurrae, Histriones: Entertainers of the Early Middle Ages," Speculum, XXXVIII (1963), 603-619.

Ogden, Dunbar H. "The Use of Architectural Space in Medieval Music-Drama," Comparative Drama, 8 (1974), 63-76.

Piper, Alfred C. "The Parchment Making Industry in Winchester and Hampshire," Library, 3rd ser., X (1919), 65-68.

Quirk, R. N. "The Cathedral School of a Thousand Years Ago," Winchester Cathedral Record, XXVII (1958), 4-8.

———. "Winchester Cathedral in the Tenth Century," Archaeological Journal, CXIV (1957), 26-68.

———. "Winchester New Minster and Its Tenth Century Tower," Journal of the British Archaeological Association, 3rd ser., XXIV (1961), 16-54.

Radford, C. A. Ralegh. "Excavations at Glastonbury Abbey," Antiquity, XXV (1951), 213; XXVII (1953), 41; XXIX (1955), 33-34; XXXI (1957), 171.

Robinson, J. A. "The Coronation Order in the Tenth Century," Journal of Theological Studies, XIX (1917), 71ff.

Schwietering, Julius. "Ueber den liturgischen Ursprung des mittelalterlichen geistlichen Spiels," Zeitschrift für deutsches Altertum und deutsche Litteratur, 62 (1925), 1-20.

Sletsjöe, Leif. "Quelques Réflexions sur la Naissance du Théâtre Religieux," Actes du Xe Congrès Internationale de Linguistique et Philologie Romanes (Paris, 1965), II, 667-675.

Smoldon, William L. "The Easter Sepulchre Music Drama," Music and Letters, 27 (1946), 1-17.

———. "The Melodies of the Medieval Church Dramas and Their Significance," Comparative Drama, 2 (1968), 185-209.

Stackpole, Alberic. "Regularis Concordia Millennium Conference," Ampleforth Journal, 76 (1971), 30-53.

Stubbs, William. "Memorials of St. Dunstan," Historical Introductions to the Rolls Series, ed. Arthur Hassal. London, 1902.

Symons, Thomas. "Monastic Observance in the Tenth Century," Downside Review, L (1932), 449-464; LI (1933), 137-162.

———. "The Monastic Observance of the Regularis Concordia," Downside Review, XLIV (1926), 151-171.

———. "The Monastic Reforms of King Edgar," Downside Review, XXIX (1921), 38-51

———. "The Regularis Concordia," Downside Review, XL (1922), 15-30.

Taylor, H. M. "The Anglo-Saxon Cathedral Church at Canterbury," Archaeological Journal, CXXXVI (1969), 101-130.

Trencholme, Norman M. "The English Monastic Boroughs," University of Missouri Studies, II (1927), 1-119.

Tupper, Frederick. "History and Texts of the Benedictine Reform of the Tenth Century," Modern Language Notes, VIII (1893), 344-367.

Walford, Cornelius. "The History of Gilds," The Antiquarian Magazine and Bibliographer, I (1822), 25-28, 84-88, 184-187, 246-249.

Whitelock, Dorothy. "Archbishop Wulfstan, Homilist and Statesman," Transactions of the Royal Historical Society, 4th ser., XXIV (1942), 25-45.

---. "The Authorship of the Account of King Edgar's Establishment of the Monasteries," Philological Essays: Studies in Old and Middle English Language and Literature in Honour of Herbert Dean Meritt. Ed. J. L. Rosier. (The Hague, 1970), pp. 125-136.

"Winckelmann, sein Leben, seine Werke und seine Zeitgenossen," The Quarterly Review, CXXXVI (1874), 1-55.

Winterbottom, Michael. "Three Lives of St. Ethelwold," Medium AEvum, 41 (1972), 191-201.

Woerdeman, Jude. "The Source of the Easter Play," Orate Fratres, 20 (1945-46), 262-272.

Young, Karl. "The Home of the Easter Play," Speculum, I (1926), 71-86.